A COLLECTION OF MEETINGS WITH MO[RRISSEY]

THE DAY I MET MORRISSEY

DICKIE FELTON

All rights reserved. No part of this book may be reproduced in any form except for review purposes.

Copyright Dickie Felton, 2009

First published in Great Britain in 2009 by Bootle Bruiser Books Ltd.
PO Box 238, Liverpool L23 6WH

1

The moral right of the author has been asserted.

See rear of book for photography credits. Every effort has been made to contact copyright holders. Please contact the publisher if there are any errors or **omissions.**

ISBN number: 978-0-9562157-0-3

Design and layout by Sundog Creative Limited, Formby, Merseyside.
01704 876393 shine@sundogcreative.co.uk

Printed by: Printfine Ltd, Liverpool

This book is sold subject to the condition that it shall not by way of trade or otherwise be lent, re-sold, hired out or otherwise circulated without the publisher's prior consent.

www.thedayimetmorrissey.com

Each story in this book is a result of interviews conducted between December 2007 and February 2009.

I spoke to Morrissey fans who had actually met the man and some recollections stretched to the 1980s. Despite the long passing of time, I was astounded by how much fans actually remembered.

At numerous stages of 2008 I tried to pass chapters through to Morrissey himself. Not particularly to seek approval, but to let him know that my intentions for this book were entirely honourable.

And, after all, the only person who could verify every detail in this book was him.

I never received a reply.

But during his concert at the Sunderland Empire in early 2008 he changed lyrics. He sung about "high rise estates in *Bootle*". And I took that as a sign.

Dickie Felton, Woolton (near Bootle), Liverpool, April 2009

Morrissey fan Hyde Park, London July 2008

"People just follow me everywhere

and in most cases it's the same people. It's quite astonishing really and massively unchronicled.

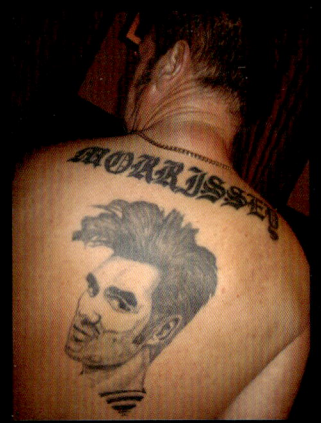

Morrissey fan Sunderland Empire February 2008.

Needless to say, if I was Madonna, which I'm not, it would be front page news twice a day. I think they just like the way I sing.

Morrissey speaking on TV in the US late 1990s

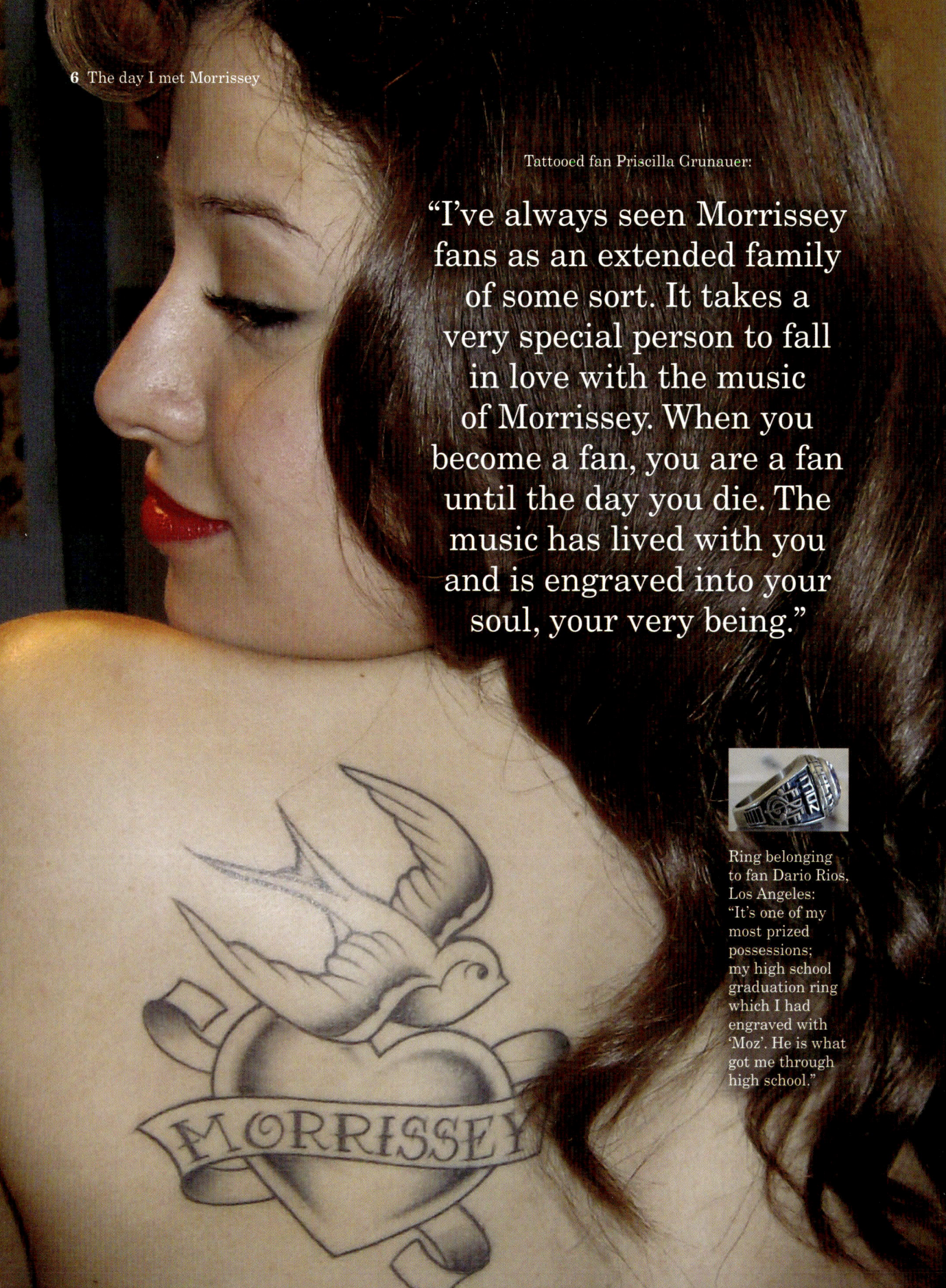

Tattooed fan Priscilla Grunauer:

"I've always seen Morrissey fans as an extended family of some sort. It takes a very special person to fall in love with the music of Morrissey. When you become a fan, you are a fan until the day you die. The music has lived with you and is engraved into your soul, your very being."

Ring belonging to fan Dario Rios, Los Angeles: "It's one of my most prized possessions; my high school graduation ring which I had engraved with 'Moz'. He is what got me through high school."

Chapters

1. **"Have you ever escaped from an Ormskirk life?"**
   Dickie Felton

2. **"Why wait for a cab Morrissey? We'll give you a lift"**
   Cheryl Morris : 1985 in Wilmslow

3. **Joy's Jesus**
   Joy Watson : 1985 in Dundee

4. **"That bloke you like is buying perfume!"**
   Sean Connors : 1988 in Altrincham

5. **"Morrissey's taking tea on the terrace!"**
   Ciaran O'Dwyer : 1990 at the Midland Hotel, Manchester

6. **"Can you find me some rare Buffy Sainte Marie?"**
   Joe Namsinh : 1991 in Pasadena

7. **"I noticed a figure at the pic'n'mix"**
   Jake Atkinson : 1992 at Woolworths, Warrington

8. **"I bet shopping's a bitch"**
   Christine Freeland : 1992 in Seattle

9. **"Famous when dead"**
   Tony Edwards : 1994 in London

10. **"You're from Eccles"**
    Johanna Wroe : 1994 in Manchester

11. **"Diana Dors Fontana 1964"**
    Danny Ibison : 1994 in Manchester

12. **The Comme des Garçons men**
    Mike Coy : 1994 in Manchester

13. **"I'm sorry but I gotta puke"**
    Jane Rodriguez : 1994 in Chicago

14. **Books and bouts**
    Steve Hampson : 1994 in Manchester

15. **"Morrissey is in my shop!"**
    Neil Houldsworth : 1995 in Alderley Edge

16. **"Excuse me, is your son in?"**
    Martin Bissett : 1999 in Bowdon

17. **Posing in the post office**
    Clint Curtis : 1999 in Hollywood

18. **"Morrissey doesn't do this for everyone"**
    Lio Monk : 1999 in Oporto

19. **"Follow that tour bus!"**
    Melinda Frank : 2000 in Nampa

20. **"Absolutely no hugs"**
    Melissa Izzo : 2000 in New York City

21. **"That one is selling like hot cakes"**
    Abrahan and Liz : 2002 in Los Angeles

22. **"The Smiths are dead, boys!"**
    Jeff Locher and Chris Sulca : 2002 in Los Angeles

23. **"I go to Nancy Sinatra's house for tea"**
    Richard Finch : 2003 at Manchester Airport

24. **"It's too hot in LA for cardigans"**
    Tom Hastings : 2003 in Los Angeles

25. **"His signature is fantastic with big loops on the R's"**
    Tom Lennon : 2005 in Los Angeles

26. **"I almost spat out my beer"**
    Iain O'Connor : 2005 in Los Angeles

27. **"Put me on stage Mommy!"**
    Julie and Winter : 2007 in Atlanta

28. **The Atlantic City Kid**
    Kyle Bourguignon : 2007 in Philadelphia

29. **"I thought I was just a trivial pop singer…"**
    Lil Morrissey : 2007 in San Francisco

30. **Hugs at the Heatwave**
    Gadi Sason : 2008 in Tel Aviv

31. **Loaves with a legend**
    Steve Barwise : 2009 in Hale, Cheshire

Dickie meets Morrissey at Manchester HMV 1994.

CHAPTER 1

"Have you ever escaped from an Ormskirk life?"

DICKIE FELTON : October 2007 : America

The 14 hour journey across the Atlantic from Woolton to Waukegan provided ample time for reflection.

The job I'd walked out on, the fiancée I'd left behind...

And what on earth was I doing 3,782 miles from home stalking a pop star?

A few days earlier I'd started signing on alongside Liverpool's unemployed at Belle Vale job centre. It was the first time since school that I'd not had a job.

I'd just jacked in a job I loathed. And anyway, Morrissey was touring America, so I thought sod it - why don't I just go?

Hastily I arranged flights, grabbed some dollars and packed my marmalade sandwiches.

I found myself on the streets of Illinois in small town America. Morrissey was playing Waukegan – about 40 miles north of Chicago. Staff at the Genesee Theatre box office were amazed I'd travelled from England when I collected my ticket.

Box office man: "We've saved a really great seat for you. We don't think we've ever had a customer fly in from England for one of our shows."

But I was starting to feel like the only Morrissey fan on earth as I strolled around the deserted streets. A solitary cop car pulled up alongside, eyed me up and down and drove off. As the weather got wild and windy I started to get second thoughts in Waukegan.

Maybe I should have caught the tour a week earlier when Morrissey played to thousands of fans in sold-out venues like the Hollywood Palladium. Instead I'd picked a quiet backwater in the middle of nowhere.

Things didn't get better when I ordered a cheese toastie at Hussey's Downtown Tavern – the waitress served me tuna. Here was me following the greatest vegetarian on earth and I'd accidentally bitten into fish for the first time in two decades.

I decided to get inside the grand Genesee Theatre early. Built in 1927, it had a massive crystal chandelier in its lobby and oozed atmosphere. But I was amazed at the spectacular 'no-show' from Morrissey's north American fans. The venue with 2,400 seats was less than half full.

Not that Morrissey seemed to mind when he marched on stage:

"It's wet…

"It's Wednesday…

"It's Waukegan!"

Despite my jetlag, it was one of the best Morrissey shows I'd ever seen (and I'd seen plenty). The fans that had turned up went wild during songs like Why Don't You Find Out For Yourself, Tomorrow and a new one: I'm Throwing My Arms Around Paris.

Security struggled to cope during the final song as dozens of fans rushed from the shackles of their seats and tried desperately to touch him.

Two nights later I was on my way to the Royal Oak Theatre, Detroit, to do it all again.

The journey from my base in downtown Chicago was the small matter of a seven hour trek on the Amtrak. I arrived weak and weary and was relieved to see the concert venue straight opposite the train station.

It was early evening and a few Morrissey fans stood at the stage door hoping for a glimpse of their hero. "You won't meet him hanging around here," I said. "He doesn't really do stage door conversations."

I was about to go and hunt out my hotel but something told me to stay. Morrissey's minder Arturo appeared. He looked about ten foot tall, ten foot wide and cut an imposing figure. It was clear something was stirring. Morrissey was near. Arturo warned me to move away.

I wasn't going to be bullied: "What? You can't tell me that I can't stand on the public sidewalk!" A moment later the tour bus pulled up. The door popped open. Morrissey jumped out and made a dart for the stage-door.

I'd travelled halfway around the world and wasn't satisfied with just a glimpse.

"Morrissey, it's Dickie from Liverpool…"

Amazingly he was diverted. He actually turned and smiled. There was no stopping me: "Will you sign my arm for a tattoo?"

Morrissey: "Well you will have to take your jacket off. I can't sign through that."

As quick as you can say Billy Budd, my jacket was

> **"He signed my arm. And I had it tattooed straight after."**

on the floor. But where the hell was my pen? Panic stricken I rummaged through my bag and finally recovered a biro.

Morrissey: "Where on your arm do you want me to sign?"

I could barely speak so just pointed. He held my right arm and scribbled. I wanted to utter something important and profound. This was my hero in front of me. My one big chance.

"Morrissey?"

"We…"

"Er…"

"We…"

"We…just love it."

Arturo then urged Morrissey away and my moment was over. Suzi, another fan who witnessed the momentous signing "session", was swept along in the euphoria: "I can't believe he signed your arm. That's so awesome."

Within a split second I was marching to the nearest tattoo parlour. Suzi watched in awe as I braced myself for the needle at Royal Oak Tattoo. It hurt.

The following morning I woke up in agony…

but it was worth it and The Royal Oak concert had been even better than Waukegan two nights earlier.

In vast contrast to Waukegan's Genesee Theatre, this gig had been totally sold out. The Royal Oak venue was smaller and it had been rammed with fans standing on three levels.

The concert had been truly magical but now my arm was killing me. And the full extent of what I'd done was starting to sink in. My mobile rang. It was fiancée Jen back in Liverpool.

"What was last night's concert like? You sent me a text message saying you met Morrissey and he gave you his autograph. That's amazing. What did he sign?"

I was in a mild panic, but thought it best to change my plea to guilty. It was hardly like I was going to conceal a tattoo from her, certainly not one that ran the width of my right arm.

Me: "He signed my arm. And I had it tattooed straight after."

Jen: "You did what?"

If she didn't already know that I was barking mad, she did now. I had my script ready just in case: "I vowed that if I ever met him again I'd ask him to sign my arm. And you know, he doesn't just sign anyone's arm. Morrissey stopped especially for me."

By the time I checked out of my bland motel on the bland freeway my hangover was kicking in. I misread the timetable and ended up sat all alone on the platform of a desolate Royal Oak train station. And it was two hours till my train.

As my arm and head throbbed I started to reflect on what it was that brought me to America in the first place. Why this popstar? I wouldn't walk to the end of my street to see Genesis, Elton John or some other crashing bore. What was it about Morrissey?

My thoughts drifted and drifted - all the way back to childhood and 1982…

School days were bad.

I'd make myself physically sick the night before the weekly Wednesday maths class. That way I could convince mum I was ill and in no state to go.

She became suspicious when this sudden bout of sickness seemed to happen every Tuesday around 7pm. But I was desperate to avoid being dragged to the front of class and slapped about the head if I got my times-table wrong.

I'd stand hiding at the back, shaking, praying that I wouldn't be interrogated.

"Felton, what is six multiplied by six minus three divided by three?" These were the days a ruler which seemed the size of Ireland would be taken to the bare legs of shaking children.

Dear old alma mater got a better aim at his quivering targets by sometimes ordering us to stand on top of our desks.

To me this was teaching at its very worst in the early to mid 19 hate-ies.

Things got marginally better at my secondary school, where you only got battered for 'serious' offences - like the time the physics master caught me singing Culture Club's Karma Chameleon during one particularly thrilling lesson on molecules and Co2 or whatever. Diving into his leather brief case for his leather strap I got an absolute pummelling. To be fair, my song choice was shocking, so maybe I deserved it.

I hated every single second of school and my continual poor grades proved it. There was the 9% score in Latin one year, the 12% score in French. And then the final indignity: aged 11, I finished bottom of the entire year.

> "That music you play is ace."
> "It's The Smiths."

In the following three years I showed some improvement but I was beginning to feel like a complete misfit, a failure and a loser.

Then one day I discovered someone else who felt the same way. Someone who had experienced the same kind of teaching, the same kind of beating.

His name was Morrissey.

It was 1988 when I was 14 and Ursula was to blame.

The girl next door. Nothing exciting ever occurred in our street. Well nothing apart from Ursula.

She was, as my dad had great difficulty explaining to me and my sister, "a punk rocker". I was mystified.

Ursula's look changed from year-to-year. Mostly it comprised of short leather skirts, ripped stockings, outrageous make-up and spiked hair the colour of which changed with the seasons. It wasn't the kind of look that was common in Ennismore Road, a quiet suburban street in Crosby, north Liverpool. I thought she was brilliant.

Our semi-detached house adjoined hers. Ursula's bedroom was about three metres of brick and masonry away from mine. Long summer days indoors meant windows open and Ursula's music could be heard by the whole street.

She played the same music over and over again. The singer's voice was distinctive, the music amazing. I didn't have a clue what it was but this was something truly wonderful. I was dying to know what it was she was playing.

So I went around, knocked on number 75, and she appeared.

"That music you play is ace."

Ursula: "It's The Smiths."

She lent me Strangeways Here We Come. Then I borrowed Meat Is Murder and turned vegetarian overnight. I related to another song on that album in particular. In The Headmaster Ritual Morrissey detailed a school pupil battered by strict teachers.

I was in love for the first time. Not with Ursula but with Morrissey.

I saw him live for the first time in 1991 at Aberdeen Capitol Theatre. I was 17.

A few months later he played my home city - Liverpool - The Empire.

There had been a slight logistical problem in me getting to that Empire concert. My stint of work experience at the cutting edge of journalism - The Crosby Herald - was in full swing. One of the reporters wanted me to experience the drama and excitement of a Sefton Council Technical Services Committee meeting that night. Yeah - right. As if. Not when my hero was in town.

Mid-morning sniffles had turned into full blown "flu" come lunchtime. Making it look like I had minutes to live, I convinced Herald editor Jane Daly that I was heading to the nearest accident and emergency hospital.

Once out of the newsroom I pulled on my Smiths tee-shirt and raced into town. I spent six unsuccessful hours hanging around at the stage door waiting for Morrissey. But they must have smuggled him in via a side door.

By 1992 my fixation with the quiffed one was at fever pitch. That December he played the Manchester Apollo. I scrambled over 17 rows of seats in a desperate clamber towards him. He'd opened with You're The One For Me Fatty and the all-seated Manchester Apollo went wild.

It was just a pity that the security staff seemed unprepared for such a public show of adoration. As fans ran from all directions to get closer, security responded and skinny bodies were smashed in all directions.

My position in Row L was about 300 miles from the stage. This was just too far from the action. As the burly bouncers got diverted by wild scenes of fandom I darted across the aisle, got myself sandwiched in the centre stalls and began hurdling seats to get nearer.

I slid unnoticed to the front, where around 300 fans had congregated to stand, sing and sway. This was Morrissey's first Manchester gig as a solo artist.

Two songs in, he played Suedehead, my favourite song ever. I had to do it. I had to get up on stage with my hero. I didn't know what had driven me to this, but I just needed to touch him. The lad in front cupped his hands and willed me to have a go.

He got a good grip of my right foot and propelled me into the air. I was like a man possessed. My left foot landed on stage.

Morrissey reached out and grabbed my hand. He desperately tried to pull me up alongside him. Then smash - three security men blasted me into oblivion. I was dragged down a dimly lit corridor and hurled into the gutter.

I did finally get to meet Morrissey two years later.

It was in 1994 aged 20 that my dream came true. For the first time in his career, Morrissey was doing the "popstar thing":

He'd arranged two signing sessions at HMV record stores in London and Manchester to promote his latest album Vauxhall and I.

Me and my mates left our university in West Lancashire at 6am and headed off to meet the messiah. Things didn't go smoothly. Pal Ian Latta's clapped out Talbot car spluttered and died somewhere outside St Helens, so we ditched it near Rainhill and made a dash for the train. We still got to Manchester before 8am - us and around 2,000 other disciples who dug in for a long wait.

At least the eight hours' queuing gave me time to prepare words for 'God' - the man whose music had given me so much confidence over the years, his voice the soundtrack to so many highs and lows.

Dickie meets Morrissey at Manchester HMV 1994.

14 The day I met Morrissey

I wanted to say something moving about how his music had changed my life, how his words had been so supportive, so defiant. Or maybe something about his idols James Dean or Oscar Wilde and how they were now my heroes too.

Such was the interest in the event, there were journalists and photographers everywhere. A radio reporter from BBC Five Live thought I'd add some colour to the story he was putting together. I was minutes away from meeting Morrissey.

BBC reporter: "I want to ferry you to Morrissey and tell me how you feel as you walk towards him. Then once you've finished, I want you to tell me all about the conversation you've had with him."

Then there he was. A few feet away. I reached him…

Me: "Er, Morrissey. Er, how's it going?"

Morrissey: "Oh, it's not too bad…"

As he signed my album, I became mute, I couldn't even tell him my name.

I mumbled: "I've got something for you…"

Morrissey: "Oh yes?"

I handled him a lapel badge which symbolised my other passion in life – Liverpool Football Club. Morrissey studied the tiny badge closely and looked bemused. And then I was out the door.

The BBC reporter seemed disappointed when I recounted the momentous meeting: "What? All you could ask Morrissey was 'how's it going?' Is that all?"

The best tour was 1999. I was 25.

Morrissey had no manager and no record deal. But he had a mad band of followers. We saw three concerts in three nights at Nottingham Rock City, Leeds Town and Country Club and Liverpool Royal Court.

Me and Latta enjoyed the Nottingham pubs big time before the opening night: Six bottles of Rolling Rock lager for a fiver. What a bargain.

When we got inside the venue - a glorified nightclub - a reporter and photographer from the NME cornered me. Or rather, I cornered them…

Me: "What are you doing here? The NME hates Moz, you've tried to ruin his career for years and here we are again it is 1999 and Moz is back yet again defying the NME with fantastic songs and a fantastic live show and you're going out of your way to kill him. Which is beyond belief."

Reporter Victoria Segal: "Well yes…"

Me: "He will always be one of the best English artists of all time and it's time that you…"

We were cut short by another Moz disciple picking up the baton in the defence of our idol.

By the time we got to the third night, at Liverpool, the concerts had got even better. They were just nights of unbridled passion and support for a man we loved. He was having a lean time and the fans loved him more for it.

I bumped into Morrissey's guitarists Alain Whyte and Boz Boorer outside the Royal Court venue an hour before the concert. By this time in my life I was working as a reporter and I handed the musicians an article I'd written about Morrissey which appeared in the Ormskirk Advertiser.

Me: "Do you think you could hand this to Morrissey?"

The gig was superb and during Reader Meet Author, Morrissey changed lyrics just for me.

He sang: "Have you ever escaped from an *Ormskirk* life?"

I was ecstatic. He must have read my article.

It was five years later when I was 31, that I had my first 'proper' conversation with him.

I was staying at Manchester's Lowry Hotel for the three-day Move music festival at Lancashire Country Cricket Ground. The

Dickie meets Morrissey at the Lowry Hotel, Manchester 2004.

event was headlined by The Cure on Friday, The Stereophonics on Saturday, but of course, all I was really interested in was the Sunday – when the main man would top the bill.

Late on the Saturday I propped up the Lowry's bar with a few beers. Somebody else saw him first: "Morrissey is sat over there."

Oh my god, I was in the same bar as him. I gulped and started shaking. I immediately dropped my Becks and ran over just as the great man was about to get into the lift.

Bootle Bruisers Joe Bullen, Ian Latta and Simon McCully fly the flag at Morrissey's Hyde Park gig, London, July 2008.

"Moz!" I screamed, "I'm Dickie. We go to loads of your gigs with our Liverpool Football Club flag which has 'There is a Light That Never Goes Out' stitched on it."

Morrissey: "Oh yes I've seen that a few times. You are one of the Bootle Bruise Boys?"

Me: "Yes I am - can I have a quick photo?"

Morrissey: "Of course."

I handed the cheap disposable camera to Morrissey's minder. Then I shuffled up close to the Mozfather.

Me: "The new album, You Are The Quarry, is absolutely sensational. We love it."

Morrissey: "Oh well, it's not that good Dickie"

Me: "I love 'Let Me Kiss You' it's the greatest song ever"

Morrissey: "Oh it's not that good."

Me: "We are really looking forward to Sunday's Move gig - we can't wait…"

Morrissey: "It might not be that good Dickie."

It was in April 2006 aged 32 when I met him again.

> "What? All you could ask Morrissey was 'how's it going?' Is that all?"

My new Morrissey banner looked the business. "Ringleaders Of The Tormentors" it proclaimed in white letters on the blood red canvas. It was ten foot by three foot. I'd lugged the bloody thing on and off three trains getting to north Wales for the first British date of his 2006 tour.

I arrived in Llandudno by mid-afternoon so took a walk around to the stage door. His coach was already in the car park, so I assumed he must have been in the building. Right? Wrong.

A gasp from a dozen lingering fans and suddenly Morrissey walked across the car park. I unveiled the flag so he couldn't miss it.

Me: "Morrissey, will you sign my flag?"

Morrissey laughed and waved a knowing finger at me.

"No. You will only sell it on E-bay!"

Meeting Morrissey in Llandudno…the moment he refused to sign my flag.

Back to America, finally a train at Royal Oak and finally some company.

I boarded and sat next to a girl on her way to a dancing completion in Detroit and a businessman from Battle Creek heading home from a Van Halen concert. I told them all about my new Morrissey tattoo and the concert from the night before.

Businessman from Battle Creek: "So let's get this straight. You packed in your job and you came all the way from Liverpool, England on your own to follow a band around America? Why?"

Me: "Well, I've followed him for 20 years. And it had been my dream to come and watch him play concerts in America. I wanted to enjoy myself and try to write a book about my obsession with Morrissey."

The businessman from Battle Creek was impressed – big time. He turned to the rest of the passengers and said: "This guy here is from Liverpool, England and he is following Jim Morrison around America writing a book about The Doors. That's so cool."

I'm 35 now. It's been 20 years since I discovered Morrissey and I'm as big a fan as ever.

There have been 62 concerts, four meetings, one stage invasion and one very permanent tattoo.

They say 'never meet your heroes' but on each occasion I came face-to-face with Morrissey he was everything I imagined he would be. He was kind, friendly, witty and fun. The problem was that in those moments I was just so humbled, so moved and totally dumbstruck.

Next time I see him walking towards me, I will dive for cover, grab a disguise or hide under a huge flag. I won't embarrass myself in his presence again.

Because Morrissey I'm sorry, I'm not worthy. This book is about the eloquent ones. The ones who've made a better job than me, of meeting Morrissey.

Have you ever escaped from an Ormskirk life? **17**

My Moz touring buddy and "Elvis jacketed friend" Ian Latta on the streets of Dublin 2004 ahead of Morrissey's Green Energy open-air gig.

Wilmslow

CHAPTER 2

"Why wait for a cab Morrissey? We'll give you a lift"

Then:
Cheryl was living in Cheadle Hulme with mum, dad and older sister Tracie (also a Morrissey devotee). At 16, Cheryl left Bulkeley School to embark on a career in the travel industry. She spent the next 10 years travelling the world with her job.

Now:
Cheryl carried Morrissey's signature in her purse for years. She took it everywhere, until disaster struck when her purse was stolen in a Manchester nightclub during a works Christmas 'do'. Her most treasured possession lost forever: "Even now that feeling of losing it still feels like a brutal punch in the stomach." Cheryl married Neil in 1994 and became Cheryl Bailey. They have three children. Cheryl is an interior designer and is still a massive Morrissey fan: "He's been the soundtrack to my life."

Today Cheryl marks the spot where she met Morrissey.

As they idled by the photo booth, the shy teenager gasped and grabbed her mum.

CHERYL MORRIS : 1985 : Wilmslow, Cheshire, England

"Oh my God, it's Morrissey. Look!"

Excited and petrified all at the same time, 16-year-old Cheryl Morris stood transfixed.

Her mum had dragged her to Wilmslow train station to suffer the embarrassment of getting photographs taken for her first passport.

As they waited for the images to develop, the unmistakable figure of Morrissey walked past. Complete with NHS glasses and long overcoat, the singer was dragging a suitcase.

Shy Smiths fan Cheryl was stunned.

Ever since she had seen Morrissey perform on Top-Of-The-Pops a year earlier she had been hooked.

That voice, that quiff, those flowers hanging out of his back pocket.

The Smiths meant everything to her. Now he was here in the flesh.

Mrs Morris was totally unphased, but seeing her daughter's excitement said: "Oh, let's get his autograph."

And suddenly, without warning, she marched after him…

"Hello Steven!

"Steven Morrissey!"

Cheryl was gobsmacked, she wanted to jump back into the photo booth in sheer embarrassment at her mum.

Why was mum addressing her hero by his first name that he never used?

The shame of it, the intrusion. Surely Morrissey would hate this?

But, as the singer waited for a taxi to take him to Hale, the conversation flowed between Mrs Morris and Morrissey. Cheryl just stood shaking, unable to speak.

Mum: "And now for an autograph Morrissey!"

He had nothing to sign other than Cheryl's still drying passport photos. Morrissey did his best to scrawl on the back of the waxy photo paper, but the ballpoint pen was having none of it. Again he tried to sign, without success. Cheryl couldn't believe she was worthy of such an effort.

She was screaming inside: "It's OK. Don't worry. It doesn't matter that the pen doesn't work. Just leave it."

Morrissey was persistent and eventually the ink flowed. Cheryl's humiliation seemed to be drawing to a close. But no…

Mum: "Anyway, Steven Morrissey, why wait for a cab when we can give you a lift home?"

Cheryl was dying inside. She prayed: "No, no, no."

Luckily, just as the singer pondered the kind offer, his taxi turned up.

Morrissey thanked them for their interest and waved goodbye.

Cheryl had escaped having to make idle chit-chat with her hero on the back seat of their Vauxhall Cavalier.

CHAPTER 3
Joy's Jesus

Joy and husband Garry about to watch Morrissey at London's Hyde Park, July 2008.

JOY WATSON : September 26th 1985 : Dundee, Scotland

Joy Watson set off for school with a spring in her step, because she had no intention of ever arriving.

For September 26th 1985 was set aside for a day of worship. It was not a day to be stuck behind a desk.

The Smiths, the biggest and most important band in the world, were coming to town and the apostles had gathered outside the city's Caird Hall.

Once out of sight of her home, 14-year-old Joy got rid of her school tie and draped granny's beads around her neck. Hair was backcombed into a quiff. She was ready.

First it was straight to Grouchos records to pick up the band's latest single The Boy With The Thorn In His Side. Then she hung around outside the venue in the hope of a Morrissey sighting.

She was stunned to see the 'chosen one' and bassist Andy Rourke loitering in City Square just outside the venue.

Joy had just the one thing to beg of the idol that walked on water.

"Morrissey...can I have a kiss?"

Just like the king who cures, Morrissey gently kissed his apostle on her right cheek.

Both singer and bassist then graced Joy's record with their signatures.

Joy: "The excitement nearly made me sick. I shook for over an hour."

The concert was amazing. The Smiths opened with Shakespeare's Sister and finished with Miserable Lie.

When the messiah hurled his shirt from the stage into the throng, Joy fought like mad to claim a piece of his cloth.

Joy had got into The Smiths two years earlier, aged just 12: "I did not fully understand the true context or meaning of the lyrics. But Morrissey's voice spoke to me and, it seemed, only to me.

"I was mature beyond my years at that age and desperate to be liked but was somewhat of an odd figure. I was tall and skinny with long features and a protruding chin. I was coming into adolescence confused and lonely and was seen as some sort of a freak.

"I knew I had found something and someone that I could identify with and I was not the only unloved freak out there.

"To me each word he sung meant something to me about my life. I was much ridiculed at school and somehow embraced it. I became vegetarian and then vegan. I followed every Morrissey and Smiths interview in magazines.

"I copied everything from vintage national health specs - with the lenses removed - to beads and paisley shirts. I didn't care what anyone else thought or said. I had my own personal Jesus."

Then:
Joy Melville Watson was born and bred in Dundee, Scotland. She discovered The Smiths when she heard strange sounds from her older brother's room. He had a bizarre taste in music: Peter and The Test Tube Babies, Frank Zappa, Kraftwerk and of course, The Smiths.

Now:
Joy still worships at the temple of Morrissey. She is married to Garry. They have a seven-year-old son. Joy is otherwise known as "Mozette".

Today Sean returns to the scene where he met Morrissey 20 years earlier.

SEAN CONNORS : September 5th 1988 : Altrincham, Manchester, England

CHAPTER 4

"That bloke you like is buying perfume!"

It was a crisp Autumnal day in 1988 and schoolboy Sean Connors was 16, clumsy and shy.

He'd just finished his first morning in the sixth form at St Ambrose College.

Pupils had been given new timetables detailing the daily drudgery of physics, geography, chemistry and maths.

Away from the classroom, lunchtimes took a familiar pattern for Sean and the lads: a stroll into Altrincham town centre, some chips, then a slouch on a bench eyeing up the 'birds' from the local grammar school.

They never actually talked to any of these girls, Sean and pals were way too cool for that. They just observed from a safe distance.

The crew loitered across the pedestrian crossing by the bus station when mate Stu Jones said: "That bloke you like is in Rackhams buying perfume."

Sean: "Who?"

Stu: "Morrissey Smith or whatever his name is."

Sean screeched: "Morrissey's in Rackhams!"

He grabbed the tape off his brother and legged it back into the perfumery with a new sense of purpose. Sean was overjoyed to see that Morrissey was still inside making his purchase. Anyway, the ice having already been broken, Sean and Moz were practically old friends.

He demanded a second signature, this time on the inlay sleeve of the tape. The autograph went right across the front picture.

As Morrissey was signing Sean managed to make eye contact. Sean studied the singer's hair to work out how his style was achieved. Then his confidence grew.

Sean: "What are your plans for the future?"

Morrissey: "Giving it all up"

Sean: "That's a big shame. I think you should reconsider."

Starstruck Sean thanked his idol, bid him farewell and then it was back to the mundane task of getting lockers for the forthcoming term.

That was it. Led by ringleader Sean they sped up the pedestrianised walkway and gawped through the glass.

There he was - resplendent in pinstriped cream jacket, white shirt, jeans and sporting a quiff to die for.

Sean marched through the doors. He approached with no real form of introduction, requested an autograph and held out the only thing in his possession - his newly acquired school timetable.

Morrissey obliged with his famous scrawl. Sean turned away and left, having barely said a word, such was his state of awe.

As he left, the schoolboy realised this was a special day: Rank, the Smiths live album, had just been released.

Sean darted into WH Smith which was 30 yards away. Bizarrely he bumped into his older brother Paul, who was walking out having just bought the afore mentioned cassette.

Then:
Sean was 16. He would later give the signed timetable away to a girl he fancied at the time who was a huge Smiths fan. Sean and pals were so distraught that Morrissey told them he was "giving it all up" they actually penned him a letter begging him to change his mind. They posted it through the letterbox of Morrissey's mum's house.

Now:
Sean is married to Catherine with a daughter Grace. He still lives in Manchester. The signed copy of Rank went missing in the 1990s but Sean and brother are busy trying to find it. He now realises that Morrissey may have been joking when he said he was "giving it all up".

Today Ciaran reflects on his meeting with Morrissey at The Midland Hotel.

CHAPTER 5

"Morrissey's taking tea on the terrace!"

Three years after the demise of The Smiths, Manchester gave birth to a music revolution.

CIARAN O'DWYER : 1990 or 1991 (it's all a bit of a blur) : The Midland Hotel, Manchester

Gone were the cardigans and quiffs. In came flares, shaggy hair and the swagger.

The Meat is Murder tee-shirts seemed to have disappeared. All the cool kids were wearing a new slogan: "On the Eighth Day God Created Manchester".

This was 1990. The city had a new sound and a new confidence. It even had a new name: "Madchester". Suddenly the city was at the centre of the universe for musical talent. Driven by the Stone Roses, it had the Happy Mondays, Inspiral Carpets, dance act 808 State and from a little further out of town, The Charlatans.

Sure there were a handful of people not mesmerised by Ian Brown's Roses and if you wanted a more intellectual Manchester sound, you could turn to Tim Booth's James.

Manchester was awash with amazing bands but one person firmly not involved in this 'baggy' Madchester scene was Morrissey. His loyal fans seemed conspicuous by their absence.

Morrissey nut Ciaran O'Dwyer had not forgotten about his hero. But he had been swept along in the Madchester euphoria. The 17-year-old would be "Avin it large" in the city's clubs every weekend.

> **"I was like a starstruck teenager. Sod accounts and their sodding faxes. I had to tell someone, anyone, everyone."**

"My job at the time was one of the best a lad could have. I was bell boy at the Midland Hotel. Centre of the economic, business, artistic and cultural world. This was where music mogul Tony Wilson had his other office.

"This was also Sir Alex Ferguson's multi-million pound deal rendezvous when he was enticing players from rival clubs to sign for his Manchester United team. The Happy Mondays used The Midland as their playground when they were gigging in the G-Mex next door.

"And who wouldn't want to work at a hotel where George Best would drop you £20 for ironing a pair of his kecks? Me pressing Georgie Best's kecks. I thought that was unbeatable. End of."

For Ciaran the only thing that could possibly be better than a brush with the football legend Best was an encounter with Morrissey.

John-the-doorman had bragged to all and sundry that "on occasion Morrissey had taken afternoon tea on the terrace."

Nobody particularly believed him, least of all Ciaran.

Anyway what would Morrissey be doing in a place like this? Surrounded by conference delegates, smarmy business men and ordinary boys?

Ciaran was nearing the end of one particularly dreary shift. Skipping up the steps from the lobby on his way to accounts, he clutched an important fax.

As he breezed past the lobby's grand piano and up to the number crunchers, he did a double take...

The quiff. The protruding jawline... Morrissey was taking tea on the terrace!

Ciaran: "I was like a starstruck teenager. Sod accounts and their sodding faxes. I had to tell someone, anyone, everyone."

The bell-boy retreated and the first person he saw was John-the-doorman.

"Morrissey's out there!"

John-the-doorman: "I know, I let him in."

Ciaran darted back to the terrace to take another look. Morrissey had gone.

The bell-boy was devastated. He felt cheated: "I needed to touch the hand of 'God' but I missed my chance. Morrissey must have gone out the back probably going to sniff out a mug of tea or a jumble sale. He must have been frightened away by the smell of corporate suits, 'hob nobbin' in the Rolls and Royce rooms."

Minutes later Ciaran's shift was over. He took off his uniform and jumped into his baggy hooded top. On came the Adidas trainers and flared jeans.

He threw his red Benetton bag over his shoulder and then it was out the staff door and onto Mount Street. Turning right into Peter Street, Ciaran stopped dead.

John-the-doorman was sharing a joke with Steven Patrick Morrissey. And on spotting his young colleague, shouted: "Here he is!"

John-the-doorman laughed as he pointed the baggy clothed waif out to Morrissey.

Ciaran couldn't move. John-the-doorman beckoned him over.

Morrissey: "John tells me you would like me to sign your bag for you?"

Ciaran was so nervous he couldn't speak. So he just nodded.

John-the-doorman, equipped for every emergency, had a marker pen to hand. Morrissey signed the bag and shook Ciaran's hand.

Morrissey: "Don't be so afraid to say hello next time I'm here. I'm just a customer."

The singer said goodbye and left. John-the-doorman was rolling around laughing. He had never seen the bell boy speechless.

Ciaran: "I must have looked a right idiot in big purple hoodie and baseball gap with curtains hanging out the sides."

Ciaran may as well have worn a whistle and glow stick around his neck he looked so unlike a Morrissey fan: "If only he had seen me 18 months earlier with my ripped jeans, patched elbow cardigan and dodgy briefcase walking endlessly around the corridors of school."

Ciaran: "But I'd met Morrissey. He'd signed my bag. He'd actually waited for me. And although I couldn't actually speak in his presence, this was top!"

Then:
Ciaran O'Dwyer got into The Smiths aged 11 to impress a girl he worked with who was a huge fan. He was bottle boy at a pub in Marple and he fancied the cleaner there. Unluckily for Ciaran, the pair's mutual interest in Morrissey did not lead to romance.

Now:
Ciaran feels his job on earth was done the day he met Morrissey. He left the hotel soon after to take up a position at a double glazing firm in a tough Manchester estate. He lasted four hours. After a seven year spell in Spain he is now back living in Manchester. He lost the signed bag. But he'll never lose his love of Morrissey.

CHAPTER 6

"Can you find me some rare Buffy Sainte Marie?"

JOE NAMSINH : 1991 : Pasadena, America

It seemed a simple enough question from the waiter in the Pasadena bar: "Can I take your order please?"

The shy star. Joe took these photos of Morrissey backstage during the 1991 US Kill Uncle tour.

Joe with Morrissey

But fan Joe was in a mild panic. What on earth would his new drinking partner want to drink?

Morrissey and his band members played pool nearby. It's not everyday that you get to buy your idol a beer.

Joe didn't want to make a bad choice and present Morrissey with the wrong tipple. Could it be a vodka or Tizer?

Luckily, help was at hand from Morrissey's guitarist Boz Boorer: "Joe, just get him a dark ale."

As Joe nervously handed the cold drink to his idol, Morrissey smiled approval and said: "Thanks."

For a few extraordinary weeks in the early 1990s, Joe Namsinh's love of rare vintage clothes and second-hand records opened all kinds of doors.

Through mutual friendship with Boz Boorer, Morrissey soon got to hear about the vinyl loving Californian kid who spent his days hunting out collectable threads and sounds.

And when Morrissey finally caught up with Joe he had some questions: "Do you think you could find some Timi Yuro or Buffy Sainte Marie records? And where did you find your jacket?"

Joe, dressed in a mint condition 1950s Levi's jacket was stunned to find himself chatting to his hero about mutual passions.

"I'd been collecting rare clothes and records most of my life. And when I met Morrissey it was just two collectors sharing information on the things we liked.

"He was impressed about my knowledge of vintage collecting and I was welcomed into the private circle and invited to hang out at some concerts."

Growing up in Montebello, California, Joe first heard The Smiths in the mid-1980s and fell in love with them. The keen artist followed Morrissey's solo career from the other side of the Atlantic never dreaming he would ever befriend the star.

It was Joe's artwork that first grabbed attention and almost granted him an early audience with the singer.

The radio station KROQ ran a Morrissey painting competition. An artistic fan that could come up with the best portrait of Morrissey would meet the star.

Not only that, the winner would have his or her work adorn the forthcoming Interlude single. Joe created a dramatic blue portrait of his idol and he won the competition.

The "winning" artwork

But success was short-lived. Because of touring commitments, the prize of meeting Morrissey never materialised and then a further blow – the winning painting was never even used on the record sleeve.

Joe's artwork signed by Morrissey

Joe: "At that time I was really sad that I missed out on meeting him and also missed out on my painting being used on the record sleeve. My heart dropped twice that month.

"But I always say things happen for a reason and if it wasn't meant to be at that time, then maybe I'd meet him at some other point…"

Fast forward a few months and amazingly Joe wasn't just meeting Morrissey, he was hanging out with him.

"Morrissey played a concert in Pasadena and as I knew Boz Boorer I was invited to tag along. After the concert I got to hang out with the band and played pool with them."

Joe went on to meet Morrissey on several occasions. The singer's band put on a rockabilly show in Van Nuys, California and Joe stood with Morrissey just watching the guys perform.

Joe: "I had many friends who were amazed that I was hanging out with Morrissey and they always asked to come along...

"But it just wouldn't have been right. I was just honoured to be in Morrissey's company so didn't really want to mess it up.

"The little time I had talking to Morrissey was short and sweet. He was very quiet but sometimes really funny. He had some great one-liners."

But what did Joe say to Morrissey?

"Well, I tried not to say too much or go and embarrass myself. I just kept it simple and friendly. I was just in awe and very happy.

"It was an amazing experience, something I can't really explain in words. I was an honoured guest invited into Morrissey's world and I hold the memories dear to my heart."

Then:
Joe was in his early 20s and hoping that his artwork would take him places...

Now:
Joe has spent a lifetime being in the right place at the right time. He has carved his name out of meeting the biggest names in film, TV and music. Joe promotes his art to famous celebrities, their signature then becomes part of the artwork. Joe: "I've met hundreds of celebrities over the years but no-one holds a candle to Morrissey. He is top on my list, my best musical artist, legendary idol and mentor. I really thank Morrissey and Boz for their friendship and kindness. Those few weeks in 1991 were among the greatest of my life."

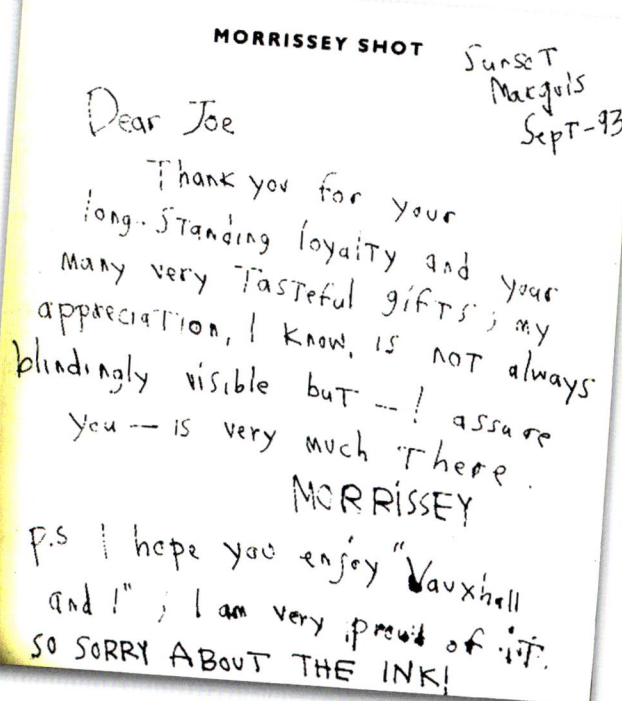

Letter from Morrissey to Joe

Tambourine signed by Morrissey and band

CHAPTER 7

"I noticed a figure at the pic'n'mix"

JAKE ATKINSON : 1992 : Woolworths, Warrington, England

Jake Atkinson spent his student years growing up in one of Britain's most famous Victorian seaside towns.

Jake's snaps of Morrissey in Warrington town centre.

Southport is "England's Classic Resort" – or so say the marketing people.

Situated 22 miles north of Liverpool, it has a pier, fairground, top golf courses and 'the smallest pub in Britain'.

On a clear day you can stand on the pier at Southport and see across the sands all the way to Blackpool.

The weather dictates that Southport is no Santa Monica, but its quaint charm and complete Englishness mean it has its admirers.

Jake was not one of them. He spent his student years in Southport. Life for him at that time was silent and grey. He was lonely, inarticulate, northern and male.

Jake: "The Smiths and Morrissey, in particular, became an important (if not the most important) part of my life in October 1986. The Queen is Dead was the catalyst and the sentiments of the song I Know it's Over seemed to be singing to me.

"I still vividly remember lying on my bed listening to the album over and over on my Walkman while staring at the sky through my attic window.

"The Smiths brought me out of my shell and gave me a sense of style. Every day without fail for the next eight years a perfectly styled quiff would adorn my head and I had a killer line in cardigans."

Jake never got to see The Smiths live. They played their last gig after he became a fan. But Jake more than made up for it. He was one of the lucky few to be inside Wolverhampton Civic Hall on December 22nd 1988 for Morrissey's first ever solo gig.

"I realised that night that I just had to meet the man."

Throughout his time at Edge Hill University (1988 to 1992) Jake was the "Moz freak". People dreaded his DJ slots as they knew what they'd get all night. When elected as entertainments officer there was nearly a riot. Funnily enough, Morrissey's people never returned his calls inviting him to play the Students' Union.

After graduating Jake realised life was going to return to its usual mundane nature.

His first proper job was running the record counter at Woolworths in Ormskirk, a sleepy market town in West Lancashire. Morrissey had just released Your Arsenal and the official store playlist of Simply Red and Michael Bolton went out the window.

Jake: "The song Glamorous Glue would regularly rattle the windows of the store until I was told to turn it down."

One day he was transferred to Woolworths in nearby Warrington. His counterpart was on the sick and there was a stock take to do.

"At the end of the dullest day of my life, I was ready to shut the counter down and clock off. I looked around the store to see how many customers were loitering and delaying my departure home, I noticed a figure at the pic'n'mix sweets aisle.

"I could only see him from behind but instantly recognised him as a kindrid spirit. He was dressed entirely in matching jeans and denim jacket with a quiff.

"Fantastic," Jake thought…"It must be another Morrissey fan like me…"

Except it wasn't another fan. It was the man himself.

"When he turned around and I saw his face for the first time, my stomach did a summersault.

"It couldn't be. Could it?" It was.

Morrissey with his friend Linder Sterling. This was an obsessive fan's dream come true. In a split second Jake was alongside his hero.

"I can't remember exactly what was said apart from snippets. He asked where I was from and I told him Southport. He made some wonderfully dry comment about Victorian seaside towns and how he liked it there.

"We talked about the Wolverhampton gig and he asked if I enjoyed it. After a few minutes it was over and I said goodbye."

Without explaining to his colleagues Jake quickly grabbed a disposable camera from the shelf and sprinted out of the store. Well, he did have to get a photo.

Luckily Linder was buying an ice cream outside so Morrissey was still nearby…

Morrissey and Jake in Warrington.

"I rushed up to him, garbled an apology about bothering him again, and asked if I could take a photo. He was happy to oblige and posed in that oh so Morrissey way; hands on hips, head turned slightly to the side and upwards, eyes looking to the heavens.

"My life was now full, it couldn't get any better." Actually, it could.

"As Linder came back over she saw the camera in my hand and told me to stand next to Morrissey."

Many people have their pictures taken with Morrissey. But how many can say that their picture was taken by Linder, his friend and personal photographer?

Three months later Jake was in London. As he walked down a street in Camden he bumped into Morrissey again. Unfortunately, away from the pic'n'mix aisle, Morrissey didn't recognise him.

Then:
Jake was 22 and had just left university. Woolworths was his first job.

Now:
Jake is living in Leicester and works in local government. He is married to Sue, who thinks Morrissey is incredibly handsome. Jake looks at the photo now and feels Morrissey looks tall, huge even. Jake believes he was literally shrinking in the presence of greatness. And as for Woolworths? Well, during the 2008 credit crunch, it shrunk too.

CHAPTER 8

"I bet shopping's a bitch"

CHRISTINE FREELAND : October 5-7th 1992 : Seattle and Portland, America

The Canadian Border Patrol officers were convinced she was a teen runaway.

The 19-year-old in front of them was dressed in black with heavy eyeliner and purple hair in a mohawk.

Christine Freeland was travelling alone and had just stepped off the Greyhound bus from Seattle.

It seemed like a straightforward plan to Christine, she would travel to Vancouver to see Morrissey on the Monday. Then travel back to the US to see his shows over the next two nights: Seattle Center Arena on Tuesday and Schnitzer Concert Hall, Portland the day after.

But the first leg of Christine's three-night Morrissey adventure was hanging by thread, at the mercy of the uniformed security staff. Border Patrol was far from impressed and didn't believe Christine's story.

They'd seen this kind of thing before. To them she was nothing more than a rebellious teen likely to be fleeing home following another row with her folks.

It didn't help that Christine was travelling light. She had no luggage, just a small purse. She didn't even have her ticket for the show as Ticketmaster refused to mail the ticket internationally.

Christine pleaded with the interrogators who stood between her and Morrissey: "Look, I'm collecting my ticket from the Vancouver PNE Forum box office."

Canadian Border Patrol just didn't know what to make of her. "Morrissey who?" they asked.

Christine: "They thought I was a runaway teen and even tried to call my mother. They seemed to think Morrissey was a made up band and eventually called the venue to verify my story."

After about an hour and a whole lot of convincing, they finally let Christine across. She arrived in Vancouver mid-morning for Morrissey's Your Arsenal tour and it was freezing. Before the concert she caught a glimpse of Morrissey and band arriving at the venue.

Christine: "Vancouver was a great show with the crowd full of energy. Morrissey was on top form and bassist Gary Day spent the show doing acrobatics with his stand-up base.

"After the show, I went to the Greyhound station to catch a bus home, but had missed the last one of the night. I ended up sleeping on the street because I couldn't afford a hotel room."

Once back in Seattle, Christine hooked up with her friend, Rob Nebeker, author of the fanzine, Morri'zine. Rob was following the whole tour that year so he could review the shows for the mag.

When they spotted the tour bus driving through streets of Seattle the natural thing was to follow. It led them to the hotel that Morrissey and band were staying in. They met Boz Boorer and drummer Spencer Cobrin in the lobby.

Christine said: "Spencer was so funny, especially recounting how nervous they were for their first appearance on The Tonight Show and how the band made the best of a bit of rest and relaxation in Hawaii."

The fans then waited outside in a hope of seeing Morrissey. Eventually he appeared.

Rob: "Morrissey, could we have a few minutes?"

Morrissey: "Of course".

Rob and a few other fans took turns posing for photos, getting autographs and exchanging a few words. But Christine froze and just watched. The star-struck fan was overcome.

The first thing she noticed was his eyes: "They were amazing. Not green, or blue, or brown, but sort of an abstract painting of all three."

Christine didn't care about getting a photo or autographs.

But she did have one request: "Morrissey, can I hug you?"

Morrissey: "Of course".

He was taller than Christine had imagined and even though she was on tip toes her chin couldn't quite reach high enough.

"My nose got stuck under the collar of his jacket, inhaling his strong cologne. Morrissey hugged me very tightly and rested his head on top of mine."

Morrissey then climbed into a car to speed him to the concert.

As he left and suddenly snapping out of her daze, Christine shouted the first thing that came to mind: "Wherever you go, I will follow you."

She didn't intend to sound like a stalker. All Christine was trying to say that she was a fan for life.

Morrissey was already on stage by the time Christine and Rob made it back to Seattle's Center Arena.

"I was so high on adrenaline I didn't care that we were so far away from the stage. It was a pretty awful show. Seattle was at the pinnacle of the grunge movement and everyone wanted to crowd-surf or slam-dance.

"Someone threw a shoe on stage which hit Boz Boorer's hand and cut his fingers. Morrissey said something angry to the audience and left the stage half way through the set. The show ended early. Everyone was pissed off, but I was still on cloud nine."

The next day, Christine and Rob drove down to Portland for show number three. On the way, they stopped at Seattle airport to pick up Christine's pen pal, Eric from Colorado.

The three got to Portland and started wandering around the streets in anticipation of the third Morrissey show in as many nights. Again they bumped into drummer Spencer Cobrin.

Spencer told them that Morrissey was in Nordstrom's department store. Nordstrom's covered a whole city block and was five floors high, so the chances of finding Morrissey inside were extremely slim.

But as soon as the fans walked through the doors to their amazement they spotted Morrissey at the fragrance counter, whiffing bottles of cologne. Christine's heart was pounding. She composed herself and calmly walked over.

Morrissey: "Hello Christine."

She was stunned that he remembered her name. They talked a bit about the show the night before, and then Christine stepped aside and said: "I'd like you to meet my friend Eric…

"Eric, this is Morrissey…

"Morrissey, this is Eric…"

As soon as she said it Christine realised how bizarre it was that she was introducing her friend to her absolute hero in such a casual way. Morrissey held out his hand: "Nice to meet you, Eric."

Christine and Morrissey were in conversation for the next half hour.

Recalling Morrissey's cologne from the night before, when she hugged her idol, Christine asked: "What scent do you wear?"

Morrissey went into a long description about how the cologne was hand-mixed by a little shop in Camden Market in London. He gave a great deal of description about what tube stop it was near, the streets, and the shops around the perfumery.

Morrissey: "I get a custom mix number 84".

He repeated it several times "number 84".

Morrissey: "You have no idea what I'm talking about, do you?"

Christine: "No, I've never been to London"

Christine was just happy to hear Morrissey talk. He could have been reciting tax statements and she would have been just as interested.

Morrissey: "Well, it makes more sense if you've been there."

Suddenly the peace was shattered by two other fans who spotted Morrissey and began running and screaming towards the perfume counter.

Christine whispered in Morrissey's ear: "I bet shopping's a bitch".

Morrissey whispered back: "Ah, but isn't life…"

Then:
In 1992 Christine was 19 and a student at the University of Washington. She was studying English Literature.

Now:
She rates the three days following Morrissey in October 1992 as the best three days of her life. To this day she is still haunted and teased by the line: "Wherever you go, I will follow you". Christine works as a data analyst. Although she still lives in Seattle, Christine has also spent time in Poland and Belgium. She's been to 32 Morrissey shows in four countries. In 2008, Christine came back to Camden on vacation. Despite an epic search, she couldn't find the perfumery that Morrissey had told her about 16 years previously.

Tony is back row fourth from the left. The person in check shirt is Murray Chalmers who handled Morrissey's PR for a time.

TONY EDWARDS : March 16th 1994 : HMV, Oxford Street, London, England

CHAPTER 9

"Famous when dead"

For two long hours Tony Edwards was in touching distance of Morrissey.

> He was so close he could even make out the wording on the singer's tiny pin badge. "Famous When Dead".

That day thousands did get to touch Morrissey. This was March 1994 and the first of two signing sessions in the UK to promote the Vauxhall and I album.

HMV stores in London and Manchester were besieged with a legion of worshippers as fans and security struggled to cope.

The events were remarkable in so many ways. It meant if you were prepared to queue long enough (some fans slept on the street overnight), you were virtually guaranteed an audience with Morrissey.

This was the first time ever that the singer had opted to meet his fans in such a public way.

Sure there were the concerts, which in the early 90s, were always advertised as "Morrissey In Person" on billboards; but this was the first time that he opted for an official signing session in the UK.

In a way it was Morrissey like you'd never seen him before. He was actually doing the "popstar thing".

industry was at fever pitch. Minutes before the session started Morrissey breezed in through a side door with his friend, Jake, in tow.

Tony: "I have to say Morrissey didn't disappoint at all. When he arrived he immediately had everyone cleared from the backstage 'green' room where myself and several other EMI staff were waiting. It was amazing how many EMI employees suddenly appeared in London that day.

"I stood on the side of the stage while Morrissey signed autographs for around two hours, still not knowing if I'd actually get a chance to meet him. As I was there in a work capacity, I couldn't really jump in and grab an autograph however strong the temptation was.

"I'd actually given my wife my copy of Vauxhall and asked her to queue for an autograph just in case. Sadly the signing finished before she got anywhere near the front of an impossibly long line of fans."

It looked like all was lost. But on returning to the green room Tony found Morrissey still there along with several EMI staff.

"I was delighted. They were lining up an official snap for the record company so I dived in. It was great. I was stood in a line-up with Morrissey for an official photograph!"

Several thousand fans turned up each day ready for a brush with their king. For many this was to be the greatest day of their lives.

Tony was struggling though. As an EMI Records employee he was technically on duty. Despite being a huge fan he was not allowed to let his excitement boil over.

It had been tough for Tony, in the ten years working at EMI, he'd never got to meet Morrissey. And that was desperately unlucky considering that the singer was on the label for several years.

Tony: "This proves how elusive he was in those days. You'd bump into far bigger stars coming out of the canteen at EMI offices."

On the day Moz was scheduled to appear in London, interest from both within and outside the record

Then:
Tony was working for EMI as an area account manager. He was living in London. He's not sure that his experience equates to a meeting as he never spoke to Morrissey. But the photograph is his reminder of a remarkable day. Tony did eventually get Morrissey's signature. An EMI official took Tony's album to a meeting she had with the star.

Now:
Just like someone else, Tony got sick of the long English winters and moved to sunnier and more relaxed climes. He is living in Perth, Australia and working as a marketing manager.

CHAPTER 10

"You're from Eccles"

Just like the thousands of other disciples, Johanna Wroe knew that today was the day.

JOHANNA WROE : March 17th, 1994 : HMV, Market Street, Manchester, England

March 17th 1994,
HMV Manchester:
The day you actually
got to meet Morrissey.

She wangled her way out of work and got herself in the queue of all queues for Morrissey's signing session. It was cold, freezing even. Johanna could feel her toes almost dropping off as she prepared to "dig in" for a very long wait.

As she got closer and closer she watched fans hug, kiss and chat to Morrissey. After seven tortuous hours she finally made it to the front. It was Johanna's turn. Clutching her vinyl copy of Vauxhall and I, she shuffled forward. The time had finally come.

Johanna: "I've waited 11 years for this moment."

Morrissey: "Have you really?"

Johanna: "Can I touch you?"

It seemed respectful to ask and she placed her arm on his jacket shoulder.

But before Johanna attempted to get closer, Morrissey looked her straight in the eyes…

Morrissey: "I know you."

Johanna: "Excuse me?"

Morrissey: "You're from Eccles aren't you? I know you."

Johanna: "How do you know that?"

Morrissey, laughing: "I'm not going to tell you!"

How on earth could Morrissey know her?

Morrissey said it again: "You're from Eccles, aren't you? I know you."

Johanna: "How?"

Morrissey: "I'm not telling!"

She had to know.

Even more bizarre when Morrissey signed her album, he spelt Johanna correctly. A split second later it was over. She was marched out a back door onto the street.

For the last 15 years Johanna has tried to figure out how Morrissey could have known her. Despite contacting different members of his band, several DJs and writers with links to the great man, she is still searching for the answer.

"Can you imagine? I'd worshipped him for years. And for my hero to tell me he knows me. I can't go to my grave not knowing. But how on earth can I find out?"

Then:
Johanna was 26, working for Royal Bank of Scotland and living in Eccles, Manchester. A few years earlier Johanna had gained some notoriety for performance poetry. She had performed one of her poems on Granada, her local TV channel. "The New Adult" was all about reaching adulthood and included the lines: "It's still freaking to the Smiths in the Ritz" and "No more happy times to remember, just blackouts in the Hacienda". Could Morrissey have seen Johanna on TV?

Now:
Johanna is married with a young family. She works in business finance. Her two children, aged six and three, have been listening to Morrissey since the day they were born. They love him as much as their mum does. Daughter Gabriella did mum proud at a Lowry exhibition recently when there were photos of various Mancunian icons on the walls: "Mummy, there's Morrissey!" she said (in the living room of the family's Glossop home is a limited edition Stephen Wright photo of The Smiths). And Johanna's take on what Morrissey means to her today?: "His words still save my life."

CHAPTER 11

"Diana Dors Fontana 1964"

Fan Danny Ibison had stored up a rather unusual question for his hero and the official signing session provided the opportunity.

DANNY IBISON : March 17th, 1994 : HMV, Market Street, Manchester, England

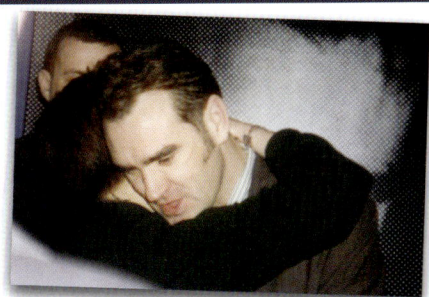

Morrissey: "Hello. What is your name?"

Danny: "I'm Danny. Morrissey, I've always wanted to ask you about a song played on your intro tape before you come on stage. It's a female singer and it's a remarkable song.

"Do you know which one I'm on about?"

Morrissey, clearly struggling with a croaky voice, spluttered: "Diana Dors - Fontana -1964."

Danny: "Er are you OK?"

Morrissey: "No. I'm not OK."

Within an instant the conversation was over. As Danny left he took a photo of the singer.

Danny: "He looked at me in a way that has haunted me ever since and not in a particularly good way. Meeting Morrissey was hardly a dream-like experience but I did get to talk to him.

"And he did tell me he wasn't feeling very well. Which is kind of how you'd hope Morrissey would be really."

Then:
In 1994 Danny was 23, living in Stockport and training to be a nurse.

Danny got into The Smiths after seeing them on The Chart Show doing Panic: "I always loved rock'n'roll and The Smiths used 50s-styled imagery. Here was a modern band clearly influenced by all that stuff so I just fell in love. Plus they irritated my family so at last I had a very belated rebellion going on." Dan was playing The Queen Is Dead LP one day but mum was unimpressed: "Not while we're eating, Dan."

Now:
Danny lives in Whalley Range. He's worked as a psychiatric nurse for 12 years. On another occasion Danny thought he saw Morrissey strolling through Manchester city centre. Danny followed the figure for a few minutes before receiving conclusive proof that it wasn't Morrissey. The man bought a hamburger.

CHAPTER 12

The Comme des Garçons men

MIKE COY : March 17th 1994 : HMV, Market Street, Manchester, England

A twitch of the upstairs curtains, was it him? Was he hiding?

Mike and Morrissey talk about shirts at Manchester HMV March 1994

Mike's son Gabriel in Morrissey pose.

Fan Mike Coy stood shyly on the doorstep:

"Is Steven in? Steven Morrissey?"

"Who is asking?" said the woman who opened the door.

"I'm Mike. I'm a great fan of his. Would it be possible to get him to sign a book I have brought along?"

"I'm Morrissey's mum. If you would leave the book, I will get him to sign it and you may come back to collect."

One week later Mike returned for the book. True to her word, Morrissey's mother had arranged for a signature.

And emblazoned in capitals across the cover in blue crayon:

"MICHAEL WITH LOVE & LONGING MORRISSEY"

It was five years later before Mike actually got to speak to Morrissey.

And when he got to his hero's Manchester HMV signing session the pair talked about clothes and not the twitching curtains from 1989.

For the shirt on Mike's back was something Morrissey was familiar with.

The fan was a regular at the exclusive Manchester boutique La Homme in the late 80s and early 1990s. One day when looking for rare vintage pieces, Mike was stunned to see a shirt on the rack that looked exactly like the one Morrissey had worn on TV a few weeks earlier.

The shop owner confirmed that Morrissey had bought the shirt from him and it had been returned a few days later after the star's TV appearance.

Even the shock of seeing Pet Shop Boy Neil Tennant trying on a long coat next to him was nothing compared to Mike's excitement that the shirt in his hands could be Morrissey's.

And so when face to face with Morrissey, Mike wanted to get to the bottom of it.

Mike: "Morrissey do you notice the Comme des Garçons shirt I am wearing?"

Morrissey: "Yes I wear Comme des Garçons."

Mike: "I think this is the very shirt you wore on the Jonathan Ross show five years ago when you sang I've Changed My Plea To Guilty..."

Mike explained to the star about his purchase from La Homme: "When I learnt that it was could have been your shirt hanging on the rack I grabbed it and splashed out £100 on it. And it was in the sale!

"This was five years ago Morrissey when I bought this and me, a mere clerical assistant at that time."

Morrissey looked impressed, but was unable to confirm that the fan was wearing a shirt that once belonged to him.

Then:
Mike got into The Smiths from the beginning but he missed out on seeing them live. Closest he got was the Tenth Summer Festival at G-MEX July 1986. Mike was 15: "I had the money saved but I had no way of getting home. My parents did not drive, what was I supposed to do? To this day I never let my parents forget that they prevented me from seeing The Smiths."

Now:
Mike became a father in May 2008. "I had the intention to name my son Morrissey if he'd been born on May 22nd - Morrissey's birthday. However, my son is called Gabriel which is a cool name and a reference to the Morrissey song Angel Angel Down We Go Together." Mike has been to 20 Morrissey concerts in the UK, Europe and seen him play in America. "It's like being a dedicated football fan travelling to see your team - but just like football - getting a ticket is virtually impossible these days unless you cave in to the touts and ticket agencies." As for the exclusive boutique? La Homme does not exist anymore – it's now a Habitat.

CHAPTER 13

"I'm sorry but I gotta puke"

JANE RODRIGUEZ : May 7th 1994 : Tower Records, Chicago, America

The TV reporter thrust a microphone in front of Jane Rodriguez but it was all too much.

Cameras pointed as the fan faced an interrogation.

Reporter: "So you are about to meet your hero Morrissey in a few minutes. How does it feel?"

Jane, cutting short the interview: "I'm so sorry...but I gotta puke."

The poor girl had just spent an entire night sleeping on the Clark Avenue sidewalk and was in a fragile state. The very thought of meeting Morrissey made her feel ill.

Following the success of two UK signing sessions in spring 1994, Morrissey decided to meet and greet his people stateside also.

On Saturday May 7th he arrived at Chicago's Tower Records.

Jane: "I had just gotten my very first job that week and Saturday was to be my second day at work. I was at home watching the local news and the entertainment reporter announced Morrissey was to do an in-store signing. I just freaked out."

Dad was unimpressed: "You must be crazy if you're going to miss work for this dope."

But mom had other ideas and on seeing how excited her daughter was, allowed her to go.

Jane and two friends grabbed sleeping bags and headed to Tower Records where they found themselves 7th, 8th and 9th in line.

"It was a rainy cold night and it was so uncomfortable on concrete. I only managed 20 minutes sleep."

The following morning the anticipation was at fever pitch.

"I just wanted to meet him and was thinking of all the things I would say to him. I was so nervous."

When the doors opened Jane's palms were sweaty and her head was spinning.

And when she got to Morrissey she felt even worse.

"All I could do was just stand there. I froze. My friend pushed me from behind and I approached the table with a poster in hand."

Jane tried to tell Morrissey how much his music meant to her.

Morrissey: "Is it Jane with a y?"

He signed the poster and posed for a photo.

Security then told the fan to move along.

Jane began to walk away but on seeing her upset Morrissey beckoned her back.

Morrissey: "Thank you for saying all of those beautiful things to me."

And then Jane just broke down and cried.

"It was one of the best moments of my life."

Then:
Jane got into The Smiths in 1988. A girl in a record shop suggested she buy Rank. The TV company didn't edit out any of Jane's interview and broadcast 'I gotta puke'.

Now:
Jane's brother teases her for still liking Morrissey. Jane: "He still thinks it's a 'phase' I'm going through. But I don't think being a fan for almost 20 years is a phase. Do you?"

Jane, feeling queasy, with her man.

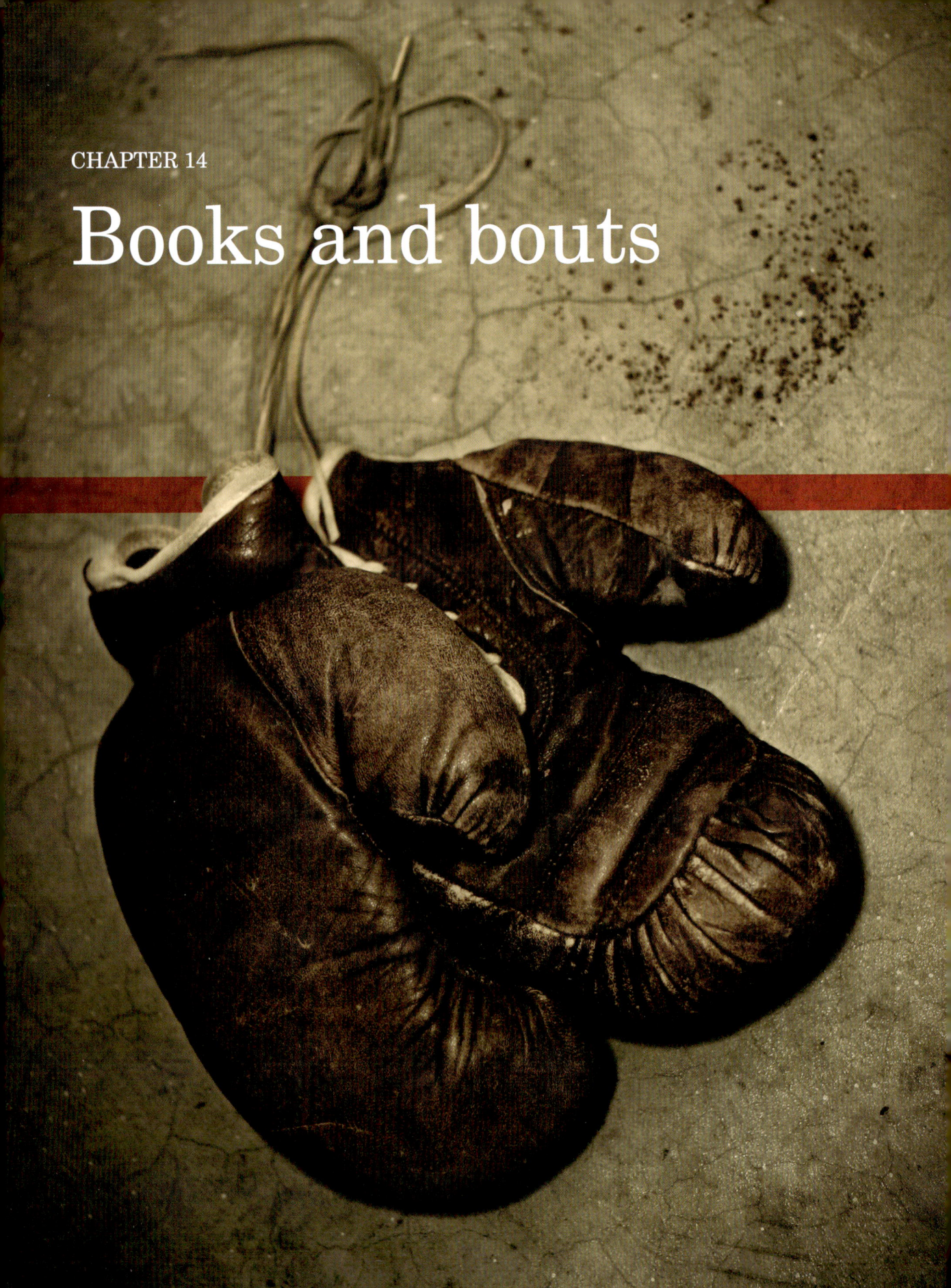

CHAPTER 14

Books and bouts

A dull mid-week afternoon, a quiet book shop and a softly spoken man walked up to the counter: "Can you tell me where the boxing books are please?"

STEVE HAMPSON : 1994 : Waterstones, Deansgate, Manchester, England

Steve Hampson was more than happy to point his customer in the right direction. His customer was Morrissey.

The iconic singer then spent ages studying various shelves. But he got frustrated and could not find what he wanted. Steve summoned the courage to go over: "Can I help at all?"

Morrissey: "Yes. I'm looking for old photos of prize fighters and boxers. I'm doing some research for a new album."

Eventually the pair stumbled upon a few relevant tombs.

Months later Morrissey released the Boxers single and World of Morrissey album. Both records contained images of boxers on the sleeve.

Steve: "When I saw that he used some of the boxing photos on his records I was really chuffed. I helped him find those images. I was there at the very start."

Five years later, Patti Smith released her autobiography and came to Waterstones to promote it. She performed a live set at the Dancehouse and Steve was fortunate enough to meet and introduce her on stage.

The following day Morrissey and Linder Sterling came into Waterstones.

Linder: "Hello Steve. Can I introduce you to Morrissey?"

Morrissey: "We know each other."

Linder proceeded to tell Morrissey how Steve had introduced Patti Smith on stage the previous night.

Morrissey: "I'm sorry I missed it. What was she like? What did she play?"

Morrissey went on to say that he had seen Patti in 1976 at the Manchester Apollo and what a great gig it was.

Steve: "I told Morrissey that I was at that gig myself. And he seemed pretty impressed."

Then
Steve worked at Waterstones from 1993 to 2000. He was 35 when he first met Morrissey and went on to see him several times in Waterstones. Once he grabbed a copy of Linder Sterling's book "Morrissey Shot" from the shelves and the singer was happy to sign.

Now
Steve works with young adults with autism and challenging behaviour. The last time Steve met Morrissey was around five years ago on Tib Street in Manchester. Again with Linder, Morrissey had just bought a Nancy Sinatra LP and told Steve how under rated he thought she was.

CHAPTER 15

"Morrissey is in my shop!"

NEIL HOULDSWORTH : September 21st 1995 : Forbuoys newsagent, Alderley Edge, Manchester

Neil Houldsworth kept up with his daily chores: re-arranging the newspapers, making sure the latest edition of People's Friend and Railway Monthly were on the shelves.

Day dreaming had been the way to get through the long shifts at Forbuoys newsagent.

He'd been a Smiths fan since This Charming Man and had always dreamt of meeting Morrissey.

You'd think that being born in Manchester and living in the city, Neil would have had a better chance of an encounter with the great man than most. It didn't work out that way. Chances came and went.

He'd seen The Smiths at Manchester's Maxwell Hall in Salford University in 1986. The following morning Neil decided to show up at the hotel where the band had stayed.

So there Neil was, waiting hours in the lobby of The Britannia, hoping, dreaming of a Morrissey moment. Things had looked promising. First Johnny Marr appeared from the lift, then Andy Rourke, then Mike Joyce, but no Morrissey.

Hopes were totally dashed when Joyce remarked: "He's not with us. He always stays with his mum when we play Manchester."

It would be eight long years before Neil got another opportunity. But what an opportunity - Morrissey's legendary Manchester HMV signing session in March 1994.

Unfortunately, by the time Neil managed to get there, he was cutting it fine. He was hardly first in the queue. He wasn't even among the first 2,000 disciples to show up.

As the queue snaked its way back down towards the Arndale shopping centre, Neil took up his position. Over the next four hours the queue moved painfully slowly. He got some distance from the main doors before security announced that the session was all over. Disaster. It looked like he was destined to miss out forever.

Then, 18 months later, came another opportunity out of the blue. The date was September 21st 1995.

Neil was working part-time in a newsagent called Forbuoys in Alderley Edge.

"I was manning the shop floor on my own. I was daydreaming, no-one was in the shop. Suddenly my eyes were drawn to outside and I couldn't believe what I was seeing. There he was. Quiff, nose everything. It was Morrissey."

To Neil's amazement, he came in: "I just froze. My heart started racing at about 100mph and I started to frantically look around for something for him to sign."

In the ensuing panic, the best Neil could come up with was a tiny postcard usually used to advertise "bicycles for sale" or "cleaning lady wanted".

Morrissey was with Linder. They began surveying the magazine shelves before their peace was shattered…

Neil: "Oh my god! Morrissey is in my shop!"

Morrissey: "So, is all this yours then?"

Neil: "Er no. Last year I queued for four hours outside Manchester HMV when you did your signing session hoping to meet you and I didn't get in…"

Morrissey: "Well, I'm here now."

Over-enthusiastically, Neil proceeded to eulogise about Morrissey's Blackpool Empress Ballroom gig from earlier in the year. He told his idol how great he was that night. Linder agreed.

Morrissey bought "Four Four Two", a football magazine featuring the then Manchester United star Eric Cantona on the front cover. He paid with a £5 note.

By this point the group was joined by the manageress who arrived from the back office. Neil beamed: "Lynn - look who is in the shop!"

Lynn looked bemused. She didn't have a clue who Morrissey was.

Morrissey: "I don't think she knows me as well as you do. And I believe you owe me £2.25."

Neil apologised, gave his idol the change and got him to sign the postcard. Then Morrissey was gone.

"Once he left I couldn't stop jumping up and down and looking at the postcard with Morrissey's signature scrawled all over it. Lynn gave me the rest of the afternoon off and I ran home to phone my mates to tell them what had happened.

"I've never felt so ecstatic in all my life and Morrissey, although probably used to this type of reaction, must have thought I was crazy."

The following year the star released a video called Introducing Morrissey. At the very beginning there is a shot of a skinhead dressed in denim, clutching a magazine. It's "Four Four Two" with Eric Cantona on the front cover.

Then:
Neil Houldsworth was 26 the day he met Morrissey.

Now:
Neil still lives in Manchester. To this day he keeps the signed postcard inside the gatefold sleeve of his Vauxhall and I album.

CHAPTER 16

"Excuse me, is your son in?"

Then: Martin was 23 and working as a junior manager at a consultancy firm. He watched Morrissey several times on the 1999 Oye Esteban tour.

Now: Martin is director at the same consultancy firm. He still lives in Manchester. He still loves Morrissey, only slightly less than he used to.

MARTIN BISSETT : 1999 : Bowdon, Greater Manchester, England

It was one of those dark, dingy, Greater Manchester days.

Martin Bissett and his mum had been driving to the hospital to visit Great Auntie Hilda who had been ill for sometime.

She was nearing the end.

The grim weather was in keeping with the poignant mood of the journey.

The drive, from their home in Rawthenstall, took them through Bowdon, close to Altrincham Grammar School for Girls.

"I'm sure Morrissey lives around here somewhere," said Martin.

Mum: "We should go and have a look."

They pulled up outside the house they thought belonged to Morrissey. They couldn't see anything other than huge gates which shut off Martin's idol from the outside world.

It still felt great to be so 'close' to Morrissey – whether he was actually home or not.

Martin had been a fan for years, thanks to his older brother who had introduced him to Handsome Devil in the mid-1980s.

His interest did not diminish when Morrissey went solo. Songs like Late Night Maudlin Street really seemed to speak to him.

And here he was, sat outside his idol's home.

Martin thought it quite a mythical place, even if only bricks and mortar.

Suddenly, there was movement behind the iron gates. They spotted a woman looking out.

A little voice inside Martin urged him to approach. She was immaculately dressed. Could this be Morrissey's mum?

Martin: "Excuse me, is your son in?"

Morrissey's mum: "Who wants him?"

Martin: "I'm a fan."

Morrissey's mum: "No, what's your name?"

Martin: "Oh, it's Martin Bissett."

Without a word, she turned and walked back up the drive into the house.

So what now? Martin felt lost. Should he wait or just leave? Was she actually going to get her son?

A few minutes passed and it felt like hours.

Then the gates slowly creaked open.

Out came a blue BMW convertible, driven, low and behold, by Morrissey.

What a bonus. Martin actually got a view of his hero. But things were to get much, much better.

Morrissey parked up, got out of the car and walked back towards Martin.

The singer shook the fan's hand and introduced himself with a bow.

"I couldn't believe it. I couldn't communicate with him initially. The last thing I wanted to sound like was some crazed fan."

For the next half hour they stood chatting.

"He seemed fascinated to learn where I had come from. When I explained I was from Rawtenstall he wanted to chat about the place. It turned out he had a friend who lived just a mile away from me in Haslingden, which was the next town. He went on to say that he had spent a lot of time in Haslingden. I couldn't believe it. I had been listening to his music for years and while I was sat in my bedroom playing his records, he was in a house less than a mile from mine."

It seemed such a bizarre and beautiful moment.

"We had a few things in common. We'd both lived in Dublin for a while. So we had plenty to talk about."

"Everything I hoped Morrissey would be, he was. I thought that he may be shy and softly spoken. He was. I thought he would be really nice. And he was. During the conversation he was very smiley. He was the perfect gentleman."

Throughout the meeting, Morrissey's mum stood close by. Martin beckoned his mum from the car to join Morrissey in the driveway.

It would have been rude not to introduce the mothers to each other.

"Mum, meet Morrissey and his mum..."

The chat turned to music. At this period in his career, Morrissey had no manager and no record deal.

A tour in 1999 had seen wild scenes at places like Nottingham Rock City, Leeds Town and Country Club and Liverpool's Royal Court. But other than the passionate patrons in town on those nights, it seemed that the wider world had turned its back on Morrissey.

His most recent albums in this period, Southpaw Grammar and Maladjusted, had received mixed reviews. The UK music media seemed uninterested.

Martin: "What's next for you?"

Morrissey: "I really don't know. I've no idea...I might play a couple of concerts in Dublin."

Martin with Morrissey.

Could he really be this casual about the music?

Was this Morrissey contemplating an end to his music career?

It felt like that to Martin.

Martin's mum had her camera. She took two pictures just in case the first one didn't come out

Morrissey: "Ah yes, always take the second picture – the safety shot."

After the photos, Martin felt it time to leave.

Morrissey: "Thank you for coming all this way to see me."

A couple of years later when Morrissey was living in California he gave an interview to Q magazine talking about life in the US.

In the opening line he spoke about Los Angeles being: "Roughly 9,000 miles west of Rawtenstall."

CHAPTER 17

Posing in the post office

CLINT CURTIS : Autumn 1999 : US Post Office, West Hollywood, America

Clint Curtis bumped into Morrissey at the post office in West Hollywood.

He stopped and shook the singer's hand.

Clint: "Man, it's a pleasure to meet you."

Morrissey: "Why?"

Clint said the first thing that came into his head: "Because you're beautiful, man."

The singer paused for a moment, eyes skyward...

Morrissey: "Yes...Yes, I am."

Clint: "Yes...Yes, you are."

Then:
Clint was stood in line about to send a letter to a girlfriend in London.

Now:
More than a decade on, Clint's post office meeting with Morrissey is one of his most cherished memories: "I remember him wearing a jean jacket and he just seemed so surprisingly tall. I'm six foot one but Morrissey seemed much taller than me. Maybe six foot three."

CHAPTER 18

"Morrissey doesn't do this for everyone"

LIO MONK : October 29th 1999 : Coliseu do Porto, Oporto, Portugal

Their wedding day was perfect and the wording on the cake said it all: "You are just like me. And your life has not even begun…"

> Porto October, 28th 99
>
> Dear Morrissey,
>
> I hope you like this photo! It was taken in July on my wedding day. The cook forgot the "R" in the word "you_r_" but... I must say it was my favourite cake that day...
>
> I'd love you to sign this photo for me! Is it possible?
>
> Again, my address is, [redacted]
>
> "When I sleep with that picture of you
> Framed beside my bed
> It's childish and it's silly
> But I think it's you in my room, by the bed"
> (who else ?!)
>
> Your Portuguese fans, Aurelio Marques
> Helena Garda

Lovebirds Lio and Helena wanted Morrissey involved in their special day.

And the best way was by putting lyrics from Yes I Am Blind on the cake.

Lio: "I wanted to dedicate a quote from that song to my wife and write it down on the cake. The cook said it was possible and we were very happy with the result."

Later that year it was announced that Morrissey would be coming to Portugal on tour.

Lio: "I was thrilled: Morrissey in my city."

"It would be my chance to see him live for the first time. It was like a dream come true after so many years listening to his songs and collecting everything about him in newspapers and magazines.

"I knew I had to be on the first row, right in front of Moz."

On the day before the concert Lio began planning for the second most important day of his life.

He made a banner proclaiming: "Morrissey, Welcome To Portugal" and then went for a haircut. The barber used his busy clippers to sculpt the word "Moz" on the back of Lio's head.

The fan also wrote a letter to Morrissey in that hope that he could pass it through to him during the

CHAPTER 18

"Morrissey doesn't do this for everyone"

LIO MONK : October 29th 1999 : Coliseu do Porto, Oporto, Portugal

Their wedding day was perfect and the wording on the cake said it all: "You are just like me. And your life has not even begun…"

> Porto   October, 28th 99
>
> Dear Morrissey,
>
> I hope you like this photo! It was taken in July on my wedding day. The cook forgot the "R" in the word "you_r_" but... I must say it was my favourite cake that day...
>
> I'd love you to sign this photo for me! Is it possible?
>
> Again, my address is, [redacted]
>
> "When I sleep with that picture of you
> Framed beside my bed
> It's childish and it's silly
> But I think it's you in my room, by the bed" (who else?!)
>
> your Portuguese fans, Aurélio Marques
> Helena Garde

Lovebirds Lio and Helena wanted Morrissey involved in their special day.

And the best way was by putting lyrics from Yes I Am Blind on the cake.

Lio: "I wanted to dedicate a quote from that song to my wife and write it down on the cake. The cook said it was possible and we were very happy with the result."

Later that year it was announced that Morrissey would be coming to Portugal on tour.

Lio: "I was thrilled: Morrissey in my city.

"It would be my chance to see him live for the first time. It was like a dream come true after so many years listening to his songs and collecting everything about him in newspapers and magazines.

"I knew I had to be on the first row, right in front of Moz."

On the day before the concert Lio began planning for the second most important day of his life.

He made a banner proclaiming: "Morrissey, Welcome To Portugal" and then went for a haircut. The barber used his busy clippers to sculpt the word "Moz" on the back of Lio's head.

The fan also wrote a letter to Morrissey in that hope that he could pass it through to him during the concert: "Morrissey had been through all that before with many other fans writing to him but I couldn´t help it. I was being honest with him and with my feelings. It was something I just had to do."

Inside the letter Lio enclosed a photo of him and Helena holding the cake on their wedding day.

On the day of the concert Lio got to the Coliseu do Porto early. Thirteen hours early.

And amazingly, he wasn't on his own.

"I had to be the first to get there. I thought if I got there by 9am it would be ok. Some fans from Spain were already there. They instantly became my friends and we talked for hours. I was amazed to see all those people there so early. At the time I didn´t know many Morrissey fans and I was so happy to talk to them and listen to their stories.

"I felt we were a brotherhood. I loved the atmosphere and it made me feel closer to Morrissey."

Among the other fans waiting was a woman who seemed a bit detached from the other followers.

"I can´t exactly remember how we started talking, but I knew she was different and I felt a great empathy for her. She told me that her name was Julia and that she had been following Morrissey everywhere since 1986.

"I bought her fanzine 'True to You' and I felt her devotion to Morrissey was astounding."

The atmosphere in the queue reminded Lio of Morrissey's Hulmerist video which contains footage of the singer's legendary first ever solo concert at Wolverhampton Civic Hall.

Lio had watched that video a million times. But now his turn had come.

"When the doors opened, me, Helena and all our friends ran to the front row. We had made it. We were right in front of the stage and very soon we'd be right in front of Morrissey."

When the concert started the fan could barely contain his excitement: "I was 27 but I felt like I was 17."

After the first few songs Lio stretched his hand through the crowd and connected with Morrissey. He handed him the letter and wedding photo.

Ten minutes after the concert Lio made his way out of the venue. A member of the tour crew came up to him and handed him an envelope.

"You are a very lucky man. Morrissey doesn't do this for everyone, do you know that?"

The fan didn't understand what was going on until he opened the envelope.

Lio, couldn't believe what was inside: "Morrissey had actually signed the wedding photograph. Everyone around me was amazed. For me and Helena it was unique and we were so thrilled."

Three years later Lio was at another Morrissey concert at the Olympia in Paris. During a pause between songs Morrissey mentioned Julia.

Lio, in his usual front row position, shouted out that super-fan Julia was "a lovely person."

Morrissey heard him and asked: "Where did you meet her?"

Lio: "In Oporto back in 1999."

Morrissey: "I remember Oporto. I was there too."

Then:
1999 was a big year for Lio. He saw Morrissey live for the very first time and married his sweetheart Helena. At that time the language teacher was using Morrissey songs in his classes to teach English (it was a cool way of introducing Morrissey to Portuguese students).

Now:
The wedding picture signed by Morrissey is framed and has pride of place on the wall in the living room. Morrissey made a mistake in dedicating the signature to "Auritio" instead of "Aurelio" but the fan couldn't care: "I really believe there´s nothing like this. I believe only a Morrissey fan understands another fan. I´ve been his fan since 1986 and it still burns. And it never goes out."

And what about that other devotee on the Oporto pavement in 1999? Julia runs a Morrissey fan website true-to-you. She has seen Morrissey live nearly 500 times. The only person who has been to more Morrissey concerts is Morrissey himself.

Melinda and pals meeting Morrissey and band.

Then:
Melinda was 26 when she met Morrissey. She was training to be a school administrator.

Now:
She is vice principal at a school near her home in Seattle. Melinda has been to 49 Morrissey shows.

MELINDA FRANK : February 5th 2000 : Nampa, Idaho, America

CHAPTER 19

"Follow that tour bus!"

The driver hurled the cassette from his car in disgust and it landed on the sidewalk in front of Melinda Frank.

The inquisitive 14-year-old picked up the battered tape from the ground. It was The Smiths double album Louder than Bombs.

"It was in a state, the tape was all chewed up but I took it home and repaired it. I was amazed that it actually played. The first time I heard the album I was unimpressed. But after a year or so I gave it another play and I loved it. And that's when it all started."

Twelve years later Melinda was ready to follow the singer on tour.

"It was easy to make friends through the Morrissey-solo fans website. So me and four other fans rented a van and went to shows in Portland, Seattle and Nampa.

"The drive took ten hours from Seattle to the third show at Nampa a small cowboy town near Boise. We looked so out of place, one of us had purple hair."

The venue for the show that night was in keeping with the Wild West surroundings – it was on a rodeo ground.

"People who turned up didn't really know who Morrissey was. And the show didn't get off to a good start. Someone threw a can of beer at him. He was not happy."

Before the concert Melinda and pals had time to kill and bought 'props' for the show: an inflatable aeroplane for the song Lost and bananas to throw on stage during Boy Racer.

Melinda: "It was just a bit of fun but I think our props saved the show. Prior to the bananas arriving on stage Morrissey looked so bored."

But as the concert went on, Morrissey got more playful. One fan lent forward to shake his hand and Morrissey 'nicked' the purple bracelet from his wrist. And when another tried to invade the stage to get close to his hero, Morrissey was impressed:

"It's the mayor of Boise!"

Afterwards Melinda and pals got in their car to make the long journey home. But the night took a dramatic turn for the better when the tour bus overtook them.

Melinda: "It was a case of follow that bus!"

When it pulled in to the parking lot of a hotel in downtown Boise, Melinda and pals dived out.

"I scrambled to grab my camera but I'd used the film up during the show. I had a spare film but I was so flustered I could barely fit it into my camera. I was shaking that much that I had to tell myself to calm down. Morrissey was so polite and signed everybody's tickets from the show."

Morrissey, in bobble hat, posed for photographs. Melinda was so star-struck she couldn't say much other than: "Can I have my photo with you?"

After the excitement was over and Morrissey retired to his hotel room, the fans hung out in the hotel bar. They needed a beer after all the emotion.

Alain Whyte later joined the fans in the lobby with his guitar and entertained them with the Smiths classics: This Charming Man, There is A Light That Never Goes Out and Bigmouth Strikes Again.

So how does Melinda sum up what Morrissey means to her?

"He has been like an older brother to me - the mentor who was older and wiser. I never really related to the theme of loneliness in his songs. But I did grow up in a very conservative Christian household and would often be told I was doing things wrong.

"Songs like Speedway spoke to me. As did lyrics from How Soon Is Now? When I went to the shows in 2000 it was my first real taste of being on the road following Morrissey and I loved it. But for me it's not really about meeting Morrissey. It's about meeting fellow fans because they instantly become friends."

Melinda with Boz Boorer.

MELISSA IZZO : October 20th 2000 : Virgin Megastore, New York City, America

CHAPTER 20

"Absolutely no hugs"

Melissa Izzo shivered on a stone sidewalk to claim the magical golden ticket that granted an audience with him.

Absolutely no hugs

The 20-year-old student had to be among the first 300 in line to stand any chance at all. So to be sure she camped out overnight.

Melissa: "The rules were that you had to purchase Morrissey's new Oye Esteban DVD from Virgin in Times Square the morning it went on sale. You were then given a voucher enabling you to meet him a few days later where he would sign the DVD."

As well as the ordeal of a sidewalk sleepover, Melissa also had to make two 400 mile round-trips from her college in Boston to New York.

She quickly organized a small team of friends with cars and figured out how many college classes she could skip to make the dream real.

The first leg of 'the Oye Esteban expedition' went exactly to plan. Melissa was number 31 in line and after an uncomfortable night, she claimed the DVD and treasured voucher.

Melissa: "I spelt my name furious with myself for not having the courage to say something witty and wonderful."

As the moment started to slip away, Melissa leaned closer.

"Thank you for everything you do. Do you think I could give you a hug?"

Morrissey instantly stood up: "Of course."

Melissa: "Thank-you."

Once she got outside she burst out crying. The tears lasted a full 20 minutes.

"Hugging him was a sensory experience in every way: his smell, his body, the fact that I was actually hugging this man who I truly loved. I spent the rest of the day in a daze, re-living the moment in my head."

She returned to the Big Apple a few days later for the main event.

"On the day itself I was a nervous wreck. We talked to the other fans around us, everyone was nervous and excited - not really believing it was going to happen."

The first 30 fans ahead of Melissa seemed to take an age talking to Morrissey.

Finally her time came.

Dressed in white button down shirt, Morrissey was sat flanked by two security men.

And they issued a stern warning to Melissa as she stood poised: "Absolutely no hugs."

Melissa: "When I stood in front of him I couldn't even remember who I was."

Morrissey asked how she spelt her name and signed the DVD.

Then:
Melissa was a late developer – getting into Morrissey in 1995. "I couldn't understand how I had lived 15 years without him. I completely immersed myself in everything Morrissey and Smiths to make up for lost time." In 1997, aged 17, Melissa went to her very first Morrissey show: "It was so positive and energizing. Very much like a religious experience."

Now:
Melissa has seen 17 Morrissey concerts in five US states and in five different countries. Melissa: "Morrissey is still a huge force in my life. I have a "Moz" tattoo, which I'm very proud of and doubt I will ever regret."

Abrahan and Liz with their idol.

CHAPTER 21

"That one is selling like hot cakes"

It was a pilgrimage to Los Angeles to celebrate her brother's birthday.

ABRAHAN & LIZ : 11.58am to 12.06pm January 26th 2002 : Los Angeles, America

And maybe, just maybe, while she was in town, Liz might get a glimpse of her all-time idol – Johnny Depp.

Liz and brother Abrahan drove into 'his' street.

Abrahan: "Maybe this is Johnny Depp's house?"

"Or maybe this one?"

They continued up the hill. They didn't see him at first - just his car. And then they sat transfixed...

Wearing a navy tank top, white shirt and blue jeans, the star loitered on the sidewalk close to his BMW.

Liz: "Oh my God. There he is!"

Not Johnny Depp but Morrissey.

Depp, one of the world's biggest film stars, shared the same Hollywood street as England's most influential songwriter.

Smiths fans Abrahan and Liz were stunned. Abrahan momentarily lost control of his car 'Brown Thunder'. The 1984 Volvo 240 DL, the fan's pride and joy, rolled backwards as Abrahan wrestled to get it back in gear. The driver's side window was half open.

Abrahan: "Hi Steven."

Morrissey: "Hello."

Abrahan parked up as his sister made for the star.

Liz: "I came all the way from Houston and never thought that I would meet you. My name is Liz and it's an honour."

Morrissey: "Thank-you."

Liz: "I met my husband Frank because of your music...And he is going to be so jealous when I tell him that I have met you. My husband had a haircut in a quiff just like yours..."

Morrissey: "Yes lots of people tell me stories like that. Is your husband with you today?"

Abrahan was frozen with nerves.

Liz: "No. I'm here with my brother. He lives in LA and I'm visiting him as it's his birthday. This is Abrahan..."

Abrahan extended his hand to Morrissey: "It is a great honour to meet you."

Morrissey: "Pleasure."

The singer pointed to a sticker on Abrahan's car.

While some drivers may have a "GB" sticker to mark their identity to Great Britain, Abrahan had a "MOZ" sticker.

Morrissey: "That is a nice sticker."

Abrahan: "Thanks. I had it specially made. I have several others too. Some you may have seen before."

Morrissey surveyed the car as Abrahan showed off his other passions. There was a sticker that read: www.theordinaryboy.com.

Abrahan: "That is my website."

Morrissey: "That is wonderful."

Then there was the Union Jack, then the Smiths sticker, then the "Powered By Morrissey" sticker on the trunk...

Morrissey: "Ah yes. That one is selling like hot cakes."

The fan laughed. That album hardly sold like 'hot cakes'.

Liz: "I watched an interview with you on MTV or maybe I read it in a magazine where you said you didn't understand why you sell out concerts in America because you are not famous or a big star..."

Morrissey: "Did I really say that? That's terrible."

The pair took some photos and as Morrissey signed autographs a Jeep Cherokee appeared. Morrissey waved to the driver.

Was this Johnny Depp?

Abrahan: "Is that your neighbour?"

Abrahan: "I got that one at the Morrissey/Smiths Convention last April. I flew from Houston to attend it."

Morrissey pointed at another one and said: "Does that one relate to a barber shop?"

Abrahan: "No, it's a skateboard company."

The fan pointed out a sticker on the back window – a cartoon charicature of Morrissey.

The star studied the image, put one finger on his chin and asked: "Is that really me?"

Abrahan searched in the trunk to see if there were any record sleeves he could get Morrissey to sign.

Morrissey: "So where do you live?"

Abrahan: "Santa Clarita, Newhall...it's sort of far from here."

Morrissey: "Yes I've heard of it. Do you listen to tapes or CDs in the car? Do you have any of my albums?"

Liz: "Oh yes we have all the Morrissey albums, Morrissey. We were listening to them on the way over here. It's weird to say 'Morrissey' to Morrissey, Morrissey."

Abrahan found a CD for the star to sign. It was the Best of Morrissey release.

Morrissey: "No. Actually that's who I was waiting for."

Liz: "Well since your ride is here, we should leave."

Abrahan shook Morrissey's hand: "It's been a true pleasure to meet you."

Morrissey: "Oh you'd act just the same if it was Weezer."

Then:
Weezer are an American indie band. Abrahan received a birthday dedication on KROQ radio two days after meeting Morrissey. The DJ said: "Abrahan is 23 today and actually met Morrissey over the weekend. Meeting your idol on your birthday, how about that?" Abrahan returned to Morrissey's house a year later and the star signed the fan's arm. Abrahan made the autograph permanent by getting it tattooed.

Now:
Still obsessed with his hero, Abrahan is back home in Houston where he works for an alternative newsweekly. And what about the wheels? Brown Thunder was the first car Abrahan bought (for $300 in 2000). The vehicle reached the end of the road a year after Morrissey ran the rule over it and was scrapped.

Morrissey and Big Jeff.

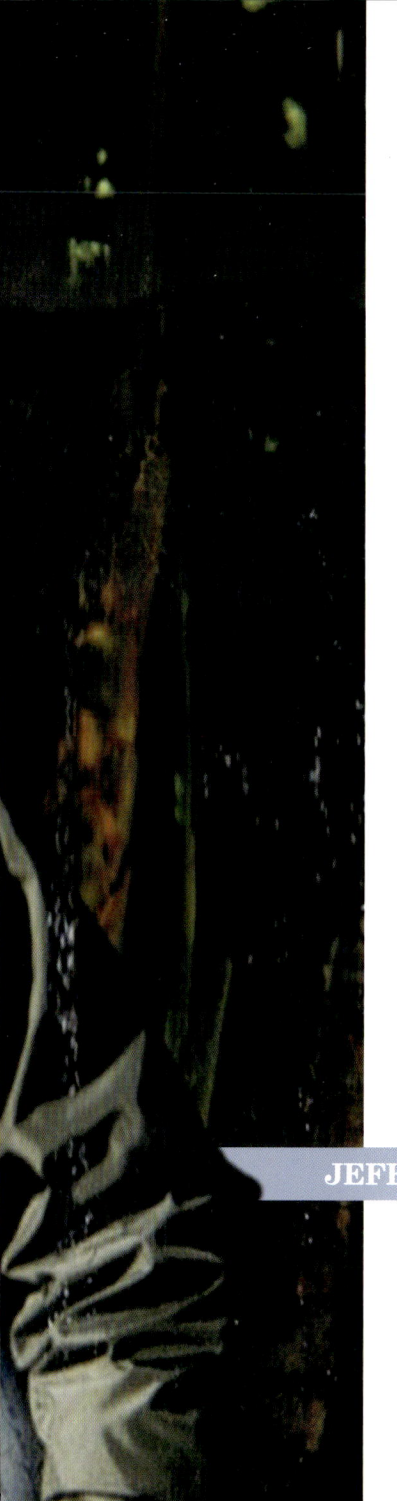

CHAPTER 22

"The Smiths are dead, boys!"

JEFF LOCHER & CHRIS SULCA : April 2002 : Los Angeles, America

They planned it like a military advance. But after a time in the trenches with no action, the troops became restless.

The day I met Morrissey

The campaign to meet Morrissey had been flawed from the very start.

Jeff: "We waited in front of his house for two hours but he didn't show up. So we left. I guess it wasn't the best idea to park our car directly outside his front door…"

Despite losing the battle, Jeff and pal Chris had been determined to win the war, and returned to the front a few days later.

Jeff: "It was a battle of nerves. We were petrified yet determined to try and meet Morrissey. We didn't even know what to say if we actually saw him. When we returned we decided it best to park farther away from his house and this time proceed on foot up the hill.

"We were in 'Operation Morrissey' mode and determined not to stop until we met him."

Jeff and Chris were well equipped with fanzines, two cameras (in case they did meet him and one camera failed), and a marker pen. Five minutes into the exercise, a sound. A sighting. Morrissey's front door opened and closed.

The great man strided to his car and the pair scrambled to action.

Jeff: "Hi Morrissey."

Morrissey, smiling: "Hello, how are you?"

Jeff: "I'm fine. How are you?"

Morrissey: "I'm wonderful thankyou."

The three engaged in small talk for a few minutes.

Then Jeff: "We're taking up too much of your time I bet?"

Morrissey: "No, not at all. Carry on."

The three stood chatting for a further 30 minutes and then an hour…

Jeff: "What about a new album Morrissey?"

Morrissey: "No new songs, I'm just enjoying life."

Jeff: "Will The Smiths ever reform?"

Morrissey: "The Smiths are dead, boys!"

During exchanges, the pair kept telling the singer how much they loved him, thanked him for his wonderful music and how much he'd touched their lives.

Jeff: "But I guess you probably hear that from everyone."

Morrissey: "I do. But it's nice to hear it from you both. Thankyou for that."

Talk got onto the current music scene. Morrissey: "Most bands are crap." The trio laughed.

Jeff: "Have you ever surfed the net?"

Morrissey: "No not really. I have a new one, but it's still in the box, untouched in my living room. I don't even know how to turn the thing on."

Chris: "I have a website called ambitious-outsiders which is dedicated to you and your music."

Jeff: "He devotes a lot of time and money to it."

Morrissey: "You do all this for me? Why?"

Chris: "We are just huge fans."

Morrissey shook his head: "You are far too kind."

Jeff: "Do you like living in LA?"

Morrissey: "Very much so."

Jeff: "Do you think you will get another record deal soon?"

Morrissey: "Oh, um. I'm not really sure. Would you buy anything new from me?"

It was a silly question.

Jeff: "Of course we would. We love you."

Despite the epic and emotional encounter the fans had yet to introduce themselves formally.

Jeff: "I'm Jeff..."

Chris: "I'm Chris..."

Morrissey: "Very nice to meet you both. I'm Morrissey."

Jeff: "We know your name. It's such an honour to talk to you. Your music means so much to so many people. You must never stop singing."

Morrissey: "Thank you both so very much."

Jeff: "I have a letter for you and a gift but I've left them at home. I forgot to bring them. Can I come back and put them in your mailbox? I mean I will understand if you say no."

Morrissey: "Of course you can. I will look forward to it. You are welcome back any time."

Despite the lengthy discussions, the fans were nervous wrecks.

Morrissey: "Are you alright?"

Jeff: "Yes. We are just really nervous."

Morrissey: "What on earth for?"

Big Jeff, all six foot six of him, started to tear-up: "We don't want to say anything to make you upset. We love you so much. We just wanted you to know how much you've meant to us."

The fans took photos, Chris gave Morrissey a sticker about his website.

Morrissey stuck the sticker under the rim of his flat cap: "Thanks, I will check out your website later."

The star signed a few things for the fans.

Jeff: "If you're 150-years-old and still touring, I'll come see you. I love you so much. Thank you so much for your wonderful words and music. They have touched my life in so many ways".

Morrissey: "No Big Jeff, thank you".

When it was over Morrissey said goodbye got in his car and drove off.

Jeff and Chris started to cry.

Then:
Jeff was 31 when he met Morrissey and was living in Las Vegas: "It was the greatest day of my life. Nothing can ever top that. Morrissey was such a sweetheart to us both. He could not have been nicer. And to allow us to come back anytime we wanted was cool. He didn't have to do that."

Now:
Jeff is a DJ and still living in Las Vegas.

CHAPTER 23

"I go to Nancy Sinatra's house for tea"

RICHARD FINCH : July 11th 2003 : Terminal 1, Manchester Airport, England

Elvis Presley, Frank Sinatra, Jimmy Hendrix... They're all in there.

Richard Finch has the greatest autograph collection on earth. A total of 370 signatures from the biggest names the world of entertainment has ever seen.

The infamous Kray twins even penned some words from prison.

Brooke Shields also sent a lovely letter. Well, she does share her birthday with the keen collector.

If you don't have a place in Richard Finch's hall of fame you aren't worth knowing.

His mum and dad got the ball rolling. Life in industrial Manchester in the 1950s was hard. They didn't have much money, but they did have imagination that stretched beyond the boundaries of post-war Britain.

Stamps were cheap and all it took was a good hand, patience and a bit of luck...

In 1959 Richard's dad wrote to Liberace and was amazed when he responded with a signed picture. Within months autographs where dropping through the letterbox of their modest Manchester home from all corners of the globe.

The Finchs' were 'all shook up' in 1969 when the postie marched up their street with a letter from Gracelands.

Richard continued his parents' good work. Having landed a job as stage manager at Manchester's Apollo Theatre in the early 1980s, he had first hand access to some of the biggest stars in rock.

One week he'd look after Dire Straits the next Tom Jones. Richard oversaw every concert from 1981 to 1984 – all 348 of them. Duties were varied. From sorting stage lights to soothing egos.

One night Richard gave Dionne Warwick a confidence boost as she suffered a bout of first night nerves. He guided her stagewards with the words: "What are you worried about? Knock'em dead babe, you'll be fine."

On another night he sped to Johnson's the cleaners to fix the zip on a pair of trousers belonging to Julio

Iglesias. Thanks to life-saver Rich, it meant the Spanish singer could be suave on stage in his favourite pantaloons.

Richard met Morrissey and the other Smiths at the Apollo briefly in the early 1980s. He can't remember much of the experience other than the band being happy to sign albums for his nephews.

His favourite Morrissey memory was to come two decades later.

Richard had long since left the showbiz life behind and was working at Manchester Airport. If the Apollo was a great place to meet musicians, so was the airport.

Richard: "Oh, I've seen them all in the various terminals, collecting their baggage or going through security or whatever."

On the 11th of July 2003, he noticed an unshaven Morrissey, dressed in black, passport in hand, ready to board a flight to the US.

Richard got yapping: "Morrissey! How are you? Where are you going?"

Morrissey: "I'm going back to Los Angeles where I live."

Richard: "What have you been doing here?"

Morrissey: "Family and shopping."

Richard: "Do you remember me from the Apollo in the early 1980s?"

Morrissey: "Erm not really."

Richard: "What's it like in Los Angeles?"

Morrissey: "It's absolutely beautiful. It's gorgeous."

Richard: "Hey Morrissey, I wish I was living in LA instead of here. What do you do in Los Angeles?"

Morrissey: "Well I live next door to Nancy Sinatra and I go to her house for tea and she comes around to my house for tea…"

Richard: "Oh give over!"

Morrissey: "No really. It's true…"

Richard, joking: "Can I come around to your house for tea?"

Morrissey: "No!"

Richard: "Hey Morrissey, there's a few things I want to ask you. My mother and father are buried at Southern Cemetery in Nell Lane. I'm sure I saw you there regularly in the 1980s."

Morrissey, grinning: "It wasn't me."

Richard: "Well what about this one: there was this girl who worked as a barmaid in the Aspley Cottage pub next door to the Apollo in the early 80s and she was always going on that her brother was Johnny Marr and all this…

"We didn't really know whether to believe her. Was she Johnny Marr's sister or what?"

Morrissey: "I've absolutely no idea."

Richard: "Hey Morrissey, did I tell you that I collect autographs? Can I have your autograph please?"

Morrissey: "Of course."

Richard: "Thanks. And next time you come through to Manchester we'll have to go for a cup of tea."

Then after a brisk shake of hands Morrissey headed to Hollywood.

Clutching another superstar scrawl in his hands, Richard clocked off from work and caught the bus back home.

Then:
Richard Finch was 55 and working as a cleaner at Manchester Airport.

Now:
Now retired and still living in Manchester, Richard sits on one of the greatest autograph collections of all time.

CHAPTER 24

"It's too hot in LA for cardigans"

Morrissey shut his front door and walked down the steps of his Hollywood home.

THOMAS CHARLES HASTINGS II : August 17th 2003 : Hollywood, Los Angeles, America

There were two figures sat on the bottom step and the singer recognised one of them: "Your face looks familiar."

Morrissey had heard of the annual fan conventions held in his honour in Los Angeles.

Sat before him was the convention's number one turn - Tom Hastings, the nine-times winner of the event's Morrissey look-a-like competition.

Tom and pal Kenny had been in Los Angeles for the weekend to visit a nightclub. After a Saturday night clubbing they crashed in their hotel room.

On Sunday, after checking out of their hotel, the pair had arrived unannounced at Morrissey's house. They waited a little while on the kerbside flicking through LA Weekly.

The pair came on the off chance and amazingly their hero was now stood in front of them.

Tom, 32, didn't want to seem like a crazed fan:

"Morrissey, I hate to be typical coming to your house like this."

Amazingly, Morrissey seemed not to mind.

At first it was conversations about the fan conventions and recording for the upcoming album You Are The Quarry. Then, Tom couldn't help himself...

"I used to have your posters on my wall and I used to always wear Morrissey tee-shirts with jeans and sport coats. I've been through all the different phases of being a Morrissey fan."

Morrissey: "Well, we do get older and we do grow up."

Kenny: "...as a teenager I would wear old thrift store cardigans with Smiths and Morrissey tee-shirts."

Morrissey: "You should get back into them."

Kenny: "I would. But it's just a bit too hot in LA to be wearing cardigans..."

Of course the only person wearing a Morrissey tee-shirt during this encounter was Morrissey himself.

Talk moved onto the concerts. Tom had made his Morrissey live debut in June 1991 at the Pacific Amphitheatre in Costa Mesa. It was the singer's second ever show in America as a solo artist.

Tom: "After seeing you perform up close in concert, it…it."

Morrissey: "It turned you off?"

Tom: "No, it turned me on. I see you as a brilliant lyricist and a very talented singer."

For the next half hour Morrissey chatted to Tom and Kenny. None of the three were in a rush to leave. The fans took dozens of photos. After a little while the Los Angeles heat began to take its toll and Tom and Kenny initiated leaving.

They thanked Morrissey for his time. As they exchanged goodbyes, Morrissey turned to them and said: "Have a nice walk".

Moz with Tom.

Moz with Kenny.

The pair could not believe it. Tom turned to Kenny: "We've just met Morrissey."

Kenny: "This is the best day of our lives."

Tom said: "Morrissey was so incredibly nice and very humble. He certainly lived up to my impression of him. I was not expecting to meet him that day. Things always seem to happen when you least expect them.

"The more I look back on it, the more surreal it seems. There were a lot of things that I wished I had said to him, but I blanked out. I suppose that is normal.

"At least I was able to tell him that he has had an incredible influence in my life. The friendships, good times and the sheer joy that have resulted from being a Morrissey fan are unparalleled to anything else in my life.

"Discovering Morrissey and his music and becoming a fan is truly the best thing that has ever happened to me. I commemorate August 17th every year - the day my dream came true."

Then:
Tom was 32 working as a supervisor at Santa Clara County Superior Court. Kenny, 30, was a DJ for college radio: KSCU Santa Clara University. He hosted his own show "One Vortex Beyond" - playing synth, new wave 80's, brit-pop and electro-clash.

Now:
Tom still works for the court as Law Library co-ordinator. He lives in San Jose. Kenny now lives in Portland, Oregon with his fiancée. He continues to DJ at clubs in Portland. The pair remain massive fans. In 2007, Tom saw 20 Morrissey concerts.

CHAPTER 25

"His signature is fantastic with big loops on the R's"

TOM LENNON : Summer 2005 : Cat and Fiddle pub, Hollywood, Los Angeles

Tom Lennon's two friends insisted he'd made a mistake.

It simply couldn't be Morrissey sat 15 yards away from them in the courtyard of Hollywood's Cat and Fiddle pub.

The three gazed on...

Yeah, it was just some dude who looked like him.

But Tom was adamant. He knew better.

Tom: "First off, the clothes: Morrissey wears a jacket where it's not required and when it's technically too hot to wear a jacket.

"And he had a really nice jacket on that day.

"He was also wearing jeans and an outstanding shirt, which looked like it was a Paul Smith.

"Not only was my hero sitting just feet away but I was dressed exactly the same. I too had a jacket on, despite it being too hot for one."

Tom was excited and itching to make a move nearer.

The sight of his idol at such close quarters sparked an intense debate inside his head.

Should he stay or should he go?

Should he ask for Morrissey's autograph? Or should he not?

The debate lasted all of three seconds.

"F*** it, yes I am going to ask for his autograph."

Tom approached trying to give off the least-creepy-vibe possible.

He got down on one knee beside him.

His signature is fantastic... 79

Tom's Morrissey signature

Tom: "Excuse me Mr Morrissey, would it be possible to get your autograph?"

He specifically didn't say just 'Morrissey' as he felt that it would have been inappropriate. Anyway it would have counteracted the "not-being-creepy" vibe he was trying desperately to give off.

Morrissey smiled and acted horribly embarrassed.

Tom: "It was an expression which said: Oh no. You wouldn't want my autograph. How sad and silly. But, yes, of course, I will oblige you."

As Morrissey signed, Tom said to him: "You're the greatest thing ever."

The fan also told his hero that he had been listening to the Your Arsenal album in the car on the way to the pub.

Tom: "He seemed to think this was either funny, or sad, or neither, but I guess it's not that surprising to him for someone to tell him they've just been listening to his record. I suspect this happens a lot to him."

Then:
Tom was 35 when he met Morrissey.

Now:
Tom is a TV actor. He plays Lt. Jim Dangle in American cop comedy Reno 911. What does Tom think of his prized autograph?: "The signature is fantastic. Strong, with big loops on the R's. It's one of the boldest signatures I've seen. I'm sure if it were analyzed, it would say a lot about him. But it's probably stuff we already know from the songs"

Tom Lennon as Jim Dangle in American cop comedy Reno 911. He sometimes wears a Morrissey shirt in the show.

CHAPTER 26

"I almost spat out my beer"

IAIN O'CONNOR : 2005 : Cat and Fiddle pub, Hollywood, Los Angeles

Like a modern day Phileas Fogg, Iain O'Connor was travelling around the world.

In early 2005 he arrived in Los Angeles; yet another stop on a year-long journey.

Iain and his mates ditched their bags at their Hollywood hostel and hit the sidewalks.

After all that travelling, it was time for a few refreshing beers.

It was a Friday night and after ten minutes wandering they found themselves at 6530 Sunset Boulevard – The Cat and Fiddle pub.

Iain was chuffed. He'd heard that Morrissey had been spotted in here before: "I've been a Morrissey fan for many moons. I've never been obsessive enough to follow him around the country or across foreign lands...

"But I'd seen him live eight times, owned all the albums, knew all the words and sculpted my hair into a bit of a quiff.

"I recognised the Cat and Fiddle as being a place associated with Morrissey although I never for a moment expected him to be in there."

Iain and gang headed inside, grabbed a few pints and went outside to the beer garden.

A few minutes later, out of nowhere, Morrissey appeared. He walked straight past them into the bar.

Iain: "I almost spat out my beer. I was so excited but I tried to remain calm."

Morrissey returned to the beer garden and sat down with three other people.

Iain: "I considered approaching him but thought he deserved a bit of privacy. I was just buzzing about how great it was that we were 'scooping' in the same pub as Moz."

Iain 'scooping' with Morrissey

Twenty minutes later, Morrissey and his friends got up to leave. The singer got within a few feet of the travellers. Iain couldn't resist this chance.

Iain: "Morrissey?"

Morrissey: "Hello."

Iain explained that he'd just arrived in Los Angeles and was a fan.

Morrissey listened intently and the conversation was going swimmingly until the pair were rudely interrupted.

Another fan had just spotted the singer and was intent on yelling her discovery to the entire world. "MORRISSEY!" she screamed at the top of her voice.

Morrissey looked to Iain: "Excuse me."

The singer gave the over-vocal fan a disdainful look before returning to the conversation.

Morrissey: "Anyway, you were saying?"

They chatted for a short while longer and when it was time to go Morrissey shook Iain's hand and posed for a photograph.

Iain: "What a start to the night! The rest was also very eventful. At one point a bouncer in The Viper Room nightclub tried to confiscate the film from my camera after I took a snap inside. This would have been a disaster with my Moz snap on it. Luckily, my dumb tourist trick worked a treat and I held onto it."

Then:
Iain was a little disappointed when he got his film developed to find Morrissey's eyes closed.

Now:
Now back from his international tour, Iain DJs at Smiths and Morrissey nights in Edinburgh and London. And as for the photo: "It's still the prized photo of my round-the-world trip even if Morrissey didn't keep his eyes open."

CHAPTER 27

"Put me on stage Mommy!"

JULIE & DAUGHTER WINTER, AGED 6 : July 20th 2007 : Chastain Park, Atlanta, America

The cheese and wine brigade hogging the picnic tables close to the stage thought they'd come to see Van Morrison.

Winter gets on stage with her hero at Atlanta's Chastain Park, July 2007

Set in one of Atlanta's leafiest suburbs, an evening at Chastain Park is the perfect way to entertain clients, or for a romantic idyll amid classical music and moonlight.

As the season ticket holders tucked into roasted garlic hummus and unfortunately meat, the tranquillity of their al fresco dining was soon to be shattered.

Chastain is not the kind of venue associated with the raw passion and emotion of a Morrissey concert. Apart from a few hardcore quiffs scattered around the venue, it seemed like most people had turned up for a quiet evening of canapés and chit-chat.

The bemused singer marched on stage clutching a packet of Cheez-Its crackers: "You've brought your dinner. And I've brought mine," he announced to the lifeless hordes in front of him.

If Morrissey seemed a bit put out by such sterile surroundings, so did Julie, a diehard fan who had travelled from Washington DC.

"When we arrived, there were a lot of people who really looked out of place. They were season ticket holders who hadn't a clue about the artist they were about to see.

"About a half hour before the show started we saw Morrissey's guitarist Jesse Tobias walking around in the crowd while talking on a cell phone. He looked irritated and sour.

"I like to imagine that he was on the phone with Moz telling him of all the disgusting meat eaters and the clueless people in their summer white outfits."

Julie and husband Karl had booked to see Morrissey ten times on the 2007 tour – at venues zig-zagged all over America. Julie made special tee-shirts featuring Morrissey and democratic candidate Barack Obama as if they were campaign partners.

She passed them to Morrissey's bodyguard Arturo hoping that the singer and band would possibly wear them later in the tour.

Atlanta was a different concert to the others, because Julie and Karl had brought along their daughter, Winter, aged just six.

Julie: "Winter's been exposed to Morrissey and his music all her life, so she knew all about what kinds of things go on at his shows. Before the concert she and I had been joking that she was going to hug Morrissey.

"I told her not to get her hopes up. I warned her that I wasn't going to let her stay up front if things didn't feel safe to me, so I doubted she'd even have the opportunity.

"We were front row centre when Morrissey came onto the stage. He walked back and forth for a moment looking us over as we all cheered.

"He looked down at the front row and when he saw little Winter looking up at him he smiled and walked over to shake her hand."

As Morrissey opened with Panic, Winter said: "Put me on the stage, Mommy!"

But this wasn't the right time.

A few songs later, after he'd finished singing Disappointed, Julie and daughter grabbed their chance.

"I thought it seemed like a good time to lift Winter onto the edge of the stage. I figured I could pull her back down with me if Morrissey or his bodyguards looked like they didn't want her up there."

But Julie was stunned by Morrissey's reaction. When he saw Winter struggling to climb up, he immediately knelt down on one knee and beckoned her with open arms...

Morrissey: "Come on... come on.

"There you go. There you go."

Once on stage, Winter hugged Morrissey and the singer lifted her to chest level and she put her arms around his neck.

Morrissey announced to the thousands: "This is my daughter! It was never meant to be this way."

Winter getting to meet Morrissey produced the loudest cheer of the night.

The rest of the concert was played out to police and security having run-ins with excited Morrissey fans. The singer seemed infuriated that his fans, his people, were getting pushed around.

Julie said: "The safety of Winter was paramount. Before the show we had put a lot of thought and care into ensuring that she'd be OK. We had seats both up front and in the back so that we could carry her back if the crowd were to get violent - which it did.

"Long before it got out-of-hand my husband carried her to a seat far from the stage and left me up front to enjoy the rest of the show."

Towards the end of the set two cops tried to move Julie from the front of the stage until Morrissey intervened by grasping her hand as he carried on singing.

Once the concert was all over Julie and husband made their way back to their car with everyone congratulating Winter on meeting Morrissey.

Julie got into The Smiths in 1987 aged 16. She had suffered loneliness and depression as a teenager and Morrissey's lyrics helped her through a difficult period of her life.

"I just adored every word out of his mouth, whether singing or speaking. I really can't overstate how much he meant to me at that time. It was a religious feeling. My obsession with Morrissey has waxed and waned many times over the years, but my appreciation and love for him never went away.

"He touched my heart in a deep way that I've yet to fully figure out. As silly as I realize it sounds, for a long time I couldn't look at photos of him without tears coming to my eyes.

"I must love Morrissey unconditionally. His music meant so much to me at a time in my life when I truly needed it that he sort of became a part of me. He's family. I have no illusions about him. I know he's an intense guy with a sharp edge to him.

"I'm also aware that he didn't write all those songs for anyone but himself. He didn't mean to help me as much as he did. I don't care. No matter his intent, he is one of the reasons I escaped my misery and grew up to thrive. For that, I'll be forever grateful."

In January 2008 Morrissey appeared at the Camden Roundhouse in London. He was wearing

the Obama/Morrissey tee-shirt that Julie had made. Julie was beside herself: "I felt like he'd given me a hug from across the ocean."

And what about the momentous moment Winter met Morrissey? Julie: "I feel that exposing children to culture, even extreme culture like Morrissey fandom, enriches their lives. It's not like we do things like this all the time. It was a unique event in her life that I think she'll grow to appreciate more as she grows up.

"I don't think childhood should be as bland as Teletubbies and the Disney channel."

Brian and Erin with son Kyle

CHAPTER 28

The Atlantic City Kid

All hell broke loose two songs into Morrissey's set at the Mann Center, Philadelphia.

KYLE BOURGUIGNON, AGED 6 : July 23rd 2007 : Mann Center, Philadelphia, America

Morrissey finished singing The First Of The Gang To Die and bemoaned the barricade that separated him from his people. Within seconds fans rushed to the stage.

As pandemonium ensued, Brian Bourguignon turned to his wife Erin and asked: "Should I?"

Erin: "Just go for it."

Brian picked up his son Kyle, held him tight and jumped over the barricade. They made it to the front.

Brian: "As soon as Morrissey saw Kyle he instantly came over to shake his hand. Kyle was so excited."

Six-year-old Kyle Bourguignon has been brought up listening to Morrissey. Dad Brian: "If my parents had taken me to see Elvis when I was a child, now I could be saying 'Oh yeah, I saw Elvis.' Morrissey is an idol and I want my son to be involved in the experience too.

"Kyle had asked me so many times to be taken to a Morrissey concert so it was brilliant to take him along with us to a few shows and make a vacation of it."

Brian, 31, of Long Island New York, has attended every Morrissey show in the Big Apple since 1991.

In July 2007, Brian and family went on the road with their idol again. After the excitement of Philadelphia it was on to Atlantic City. Again Kyle and dad made it to the front.

The youngster had drawn a picture with a note on it for Morrissey. After a couple of songs Morrissey was once again smiling and shaking Kyle's hand. About half-way through the show Morrissey came over to the side of the stage where Kyle was standing. About a million dreams came true when the star actually started talking to Kyle.

Morrissey: "What is your name?"

A few months later the family went to see Morrissey four times in a week at the Hammerstein Ballroom in New York.

On the fourth and final night Kyle handed Morrissey flowers as he sang The Boy With The Thorn In His Side. The singer was clearly moved and turned to Kyle as he accepted his flowers.

And Morrissey said: "Please don't make me sentimental."

Lil Morrissey on stage with his namesake.

LIL MORRISSEY, AGED 6 : September 2007 : The Fillmore, San Francisco, America

CHAPTER 29

"I thought I was just a trivial pop singer…"

Fan David Reyes paid Morrissey the ultimate tribute. He named one of his children after him.

And now Lil Morrissey, six, is as big a fan as his dad.

David: "Aside from becoming a father, I must confess that Morrissey is the greatest thing that's happened to me. I was lucky enough to have named my last son Morrissey and it has paid off."

David grew up in Sacramento, the capital of California. In the early years times were hard but David was 'saved' in 1992 when he discovered the music of Morrissey in the 8th grade.

"He was a saviour. I was a typical teenager growing up in poverty. Morrissey carried me through the good and bad times. So when I grew up and had children, I named my last son Morrissey.

"For the first year of his life he was only allowed to listen to classical music and Morrissey who he fell in love with."

Little Morrissey would meet 'big' Morrissey twice on his 2007 tour - in Bakersfield and in dramatic fashion at San Francisco's Fillmore Theatre.

Lil Morrissey with one of Morrissey's minders.

David and his son's dreams came true that night: "Lil made it on stage and hugged his hero, our hero."

The concert in Bakersfield was a five hour car trip and Lil and dad listened to Morrissey throughout the journey.

David: "I was so excited, not for me for my son…well ok, I was excited too. But more for him."

During the whole journey Lil asked his dad would it be possible to meet Morrissey and even sing with him on stage: "It was so hard to answer those questions because I didn't think it would be possible at all."

Father and son had seats about 15 rows from the front so the day before the concert they went to the box office to see if they could get seats nearer the stage.

"The lady at the window was very nice and made our trip. When I asked what tickets were available she told me she had a few in the second and third rows. The price was $85.00 each.

"God was present that day and she told me I could trade my original tickets. I just about died."

Things got even better a few months later when the star returned to California for four nights at The Fillmore San Francisco. David and son got to the venue five hours before Morrissey was due on stage. When they got inside they were right at the front.

During the show the singer turned to the young boy with the quiff in row one.

Morrissey: "What is your name?"

He handed Lil the microphone…

Lil: "My name is Morrissey."

Morrissey: "…and I thought I was just a trivial pop singer."

A few songs later Morrissey began singing I Like You and he beckoned young Morrissey son on stage with him. For the next few minutes the six-year-old danced and sang along with his hero.

Today Lil Morrissey is getting ready to put a Morrissey cover band together and start doing shows himself.

CHAPTER 30

Hugs at the Heatwave

GADI SASON : July 29th 2008 :

The ten fans stood in line as if they were suspects in a police identification parade.

Gadi (far left) at the Israeli Morrissey "love-in".

Tel Aviv Convention Centre, Israel

Before the moment of truth they were issued with a stern warning from security:

"When the door opens and Morrissey comes in, you must not ask for his autograph. Do not give him presents. There will be no cameras. There will be no mobile phones. Stand in line - at all times. There will be one group photo at the end. If you break any of these rules, the meeting Morrissey session will end."

Gadi Sason was unimpressed: "We were made to feel like criminals in a police line-up. We couldn't believe how strict they were being. It was very orchestrated. It was like 'Morrissey is the star and we are the fans' and the roles played out will be very clear."

The moment Morrissey announced plans to headline Tel Aviv's Heatwave festival in summer 2008, fan Gadi schemed to set up an unlikely meeting with the star.

The 36-year-old former journalist had contacts. His time editing for the Israeli Time Out and other titles such as The Pink Time (Israel's only gay magazine) had made him well connected.

A few weeks before the concert, Gadi phoned the Israeli promoter and suggested Morrissey meet some of his fans while he was in the city: "It would be good for PR," said the fan.

Amazingly, a few days before Morrissey touched down at Ben Gurion Airport, Gadi got an unexpected call from the promoter: "Morrissey has been thinking about your suggestion and has agreed."

Gadi was stunned. This was Morrissey breaking with tradition and agreeing to a fan meeting just an hour before he was due on stage. Panic ensued. What on earth would Gadi wear? After much debate he settled on a Smiths Meat is Murder tee-shirt and jeans.

When the day came, Gadi and nine other giddy fans assembled in the lobby of the Tel Aviv Convention Centre.

But before they met the star they were led to a side room and read the riot act. Gadi: "At first I thought what the F*** is this? It was frightening."

Then Morrissey appeared. Like royalty being presented to his subjects, the King strolled down the line of fans.

One was Karel Lahmy.

Karel: "I've waited for this moment for 20 years."

Morrissey: "Yeah. Me too."

Gadi Sason was the last person he greeted.

Morrissey instantly clocked the tee-shirt: "Oh, very nice..."

Gadi: "I became vegetarian because of you."

Morrissey: "I'm very honoured."

Then for the official photograph. Morrissey stood in middle of the pack but Gadi was 'miles away' on the fringes of the photo. There was nothing else for it but to breach 'the law' and break ranks.

As the photographer lined up her shot, Gadi left his position and got as close to Morrissey as possible. He sat straight in front of him. In contrast to the strict warnings given to fans before the meeting, Morrissey was in playful mood. To the amazement of everyone present, the singer grabbed Gadi and toppled to the floor. It sparked a mass 'love-in' between Morrissey and fans.

Rolling around the floor, ten fans and one very cheeky star were suddenly at one.

Gadi: "It was a lovely moment, very joyful."

But what is Gadi's general take on the moment a fan comes face-to-face with Morrissey? "I think that some fans are deluded if they think meeting Morrissey is in some way going to change their life. I think that if a fan meets him one-on-one they have such massive expectations that it can lead to disappointment. If anyone expects to have a lengthy conversation with him about their broken heart or their long lost love or whatever...it's just not going to happen."

Gadi first heard the Smiths when he wrote a review of The World Won't Listen album. But he didn't really become a serious devotee until the late 1990s.

This was a time when Morrissey was 'exiled' in LA and 'exiled' from the top of the pop charts. On seeing his apparent 'distress' some record companies were reported to have offered Morrissey deals which

would have meant him ditching his band or a fate worse than death – ordering some kind of "re-brand" of the man himself.

Gadi: "He went through a very dark period when he had no record deal. But he never gave in and he never ever sold his soul. That's when I thought this man really is a star who has integrity. That's one of the reasons why there is so much admiration for him. And so much love."

The Baker Boys: Steve and David.

CHAPTER 31

Loaves with a legend

The scene at Lake, a design agency based in Hale, Cheshire, was one of jubilation.

STEVE BARWISE : 12.55pm, 19th February 2009 : Hale, Cheshire

Employees there had won an important five-a-side football match the previous night.

Work was put to one side as football banter at the company's office flowed. The game had featured this book's author who was on the losing side.

Lake designer Bernard Hesketh joked with his work pals: "Beating Dickie and his team so comprehensively last night was brilliant. Dickie wants to spend less time writing books about Morrissey and get practising his football skills instead. Winning the game by 22 goals to four - it can't get better than this can it?"

Colleague Steve Barwise replied: "It can't get any better, but I'm starving and it's time for lunch. Does anyone want anything from the bakery next door?"

Steve popped out and walked along Hale High Street to Hills Bakery. The 45-year-old Liverpudlian stood at the till, placed his order and became aware of a presence next to him. It was Morrissey.

The singer was dressed in dark denim wearing a peeked cap and clutching two of Hills' delicious home-made loaves.

Steve, who had been a fan of Morrissey for years, was overcome with emotion: "I didn't know what to say at first, but I knew I had to speak to him. This was Morrissey in front of me. His lyrics had held so much meaning to me over the years. I view him like John Lennon. He is a poet."

So over the savouries and cakes, Steve leaned close to the Mozfather. And just like the football match the night before, he took his chance. He turned to the star and cool as a cucumber simply whispered in his ear: "Thank you for the words."

Steve was less composed on return to the office: "Oh my God, you are not going to believe me lads! I've just bumped into Morrissey in the bakers. No messing, honestly, it was him. I spoke to him."

The shock meeting sent another Lake employee, David Parry, into frenzy. He had been a Morrissey disciple virtually since birth. The young designer ditched his work in an instant and sped onto the street.

David zig-zagged up and down Hale High Street three times. Where had Morrissey gone? As the sweat poured from the fan's 23-year-old brow, he eventually gave up the chase.

David: "I had been a massive Morrissey fan for years and years. And he had been standing just yards from the office. How could I have missed out on meeting him? I was gutted and so deflated. I don't know what I would have said to Morrisscy had I met him.

"But I would have said something..."

THE AUTHOR

Dickie Felton was born in Liverpool in 1973. He finished bottom of his entire school in 1985. He went on to retake and spectacularly fail his maths GCSE six times.

Felton is a former Liverpool ECHO and Daily Post reporter. He left journalism in 2001 to work in PR. He is now media manager at Keep Britain Tidy. And he thinks Morrissey would approve.

The Liverpool FC season ticket holder lives in the same street Paul McCartney first met John Lennon to form The Beatles. But there is only one songwriter that really matters...

The Day I Met Morrissey is his first book.

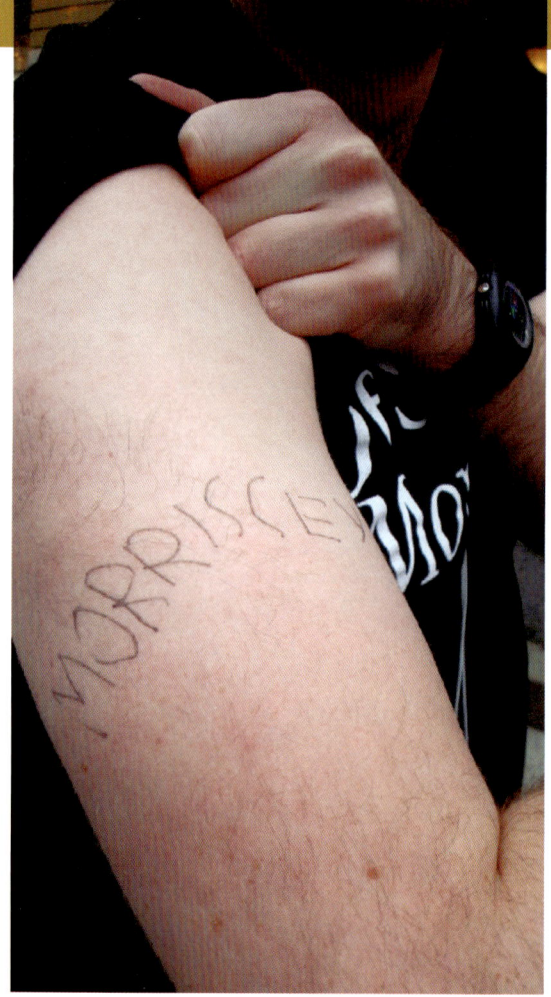

Author's right arm signed by Morrissey
Royal Oak, Michigan, USA, Oct 2007

World of Morrissey

● 8 : Seattle : 1992

● 13 : Chicago : 1994
● 20 : New York : 1999
● 28 : Philadelphia : 2007

● 19 : Nampa : 2000

● 29 : San Francisco : 2007
 ● 6 : Pasadena : 1991
  17 : Hollywood : 1999
  21 : Los Angeles : 2002
  22 : Los Angeles : 2002
  24 : Los Angeles : 2003
  25 : Los Angeles : 2005
  26 : Los Angeles : 2005

● 27 : Atlanta : 2007

DICKIE FELTON has met Morrissey on numerous occasions over the years including:

1994 : HMV, Manchester

2004 : The Lowry Hotel, Manchester

2006 : Llandudno, Wales

2007 : Royal Oak, Michigan, America

Thank you...

At the helm: Jennifer. On our first date she revealed she'd watched The Smiths live at Lancaster University in 1983 (and that really impressed me).

With special thanks to Ursula P who introduced me to the music of Morrissey. Ursula where are you now?

With love and longing to all the loafing oafs, Bootle Bruisers and Morrissey touring companions over the last two decades: Colin Stewart, Dan Gallagher, Nicola Wilford, Ian Latta, Joe Bullen, Simon McCully, Jacqueline O'Connor, Tammy Goddard, Lisa Garrett and Polly Rourke.

Cheers to David Tseng at Morrissey-solo.com, Len Brown, Fiona Campbell, Ginette Unsworth, Ian Clayton, Phil Barton, Scott Stevens and everyone at Keep Britain Tidy, The Manchester Evening News, Terry Christian, BBC Radio Manchester, Channel M Manchester, Robin Maryon, Lake, Northern Trains (most of this book was written on the Liverpool to Wigan line), and Royal Oak Tattoo, Michigan, USA.

Thanks to Omnibus Press for permission to reproduce Morrissey In His Own Words book (by John Robertson 1988).

Thanks to mum and dad who never quite understood my obsession but agreed to be 'dragged' to their first Morrissey concert at Liverpool Empire on May 10th 2009.

Dickie Felton review of Morrissey's Chester concert in The Ormskirk Advertiser December 1997.

Following the star

IT'S VERY easy to get greedy about Morrissey. The more you see him the more you want him.

And as the lights dim and the last great pop star walks on stage 2,000 fans surge forward to let the Moz worshipping begin.

Not that the passion hadn't started hours earlier. In the pub opposite the venue hundreds of quiffed up fans are exchanging tales of the night before - when their idol played London's Battersea Power Station.

Fans had travelled from all over Britain to see Morrissey and many had travelled to Chester straight from the London gig. The scene in the pub and then later in the venue is a spectacular one......

You think that you've walked straight into a scene from Rebel Without a Cause and half expect James Dean to walk past wearing a Smiths t-shirt and an excited smile.

One starry-eyed disciple says: "I've come here on my own - but you always meet people because it's a Morrissey gig." And some fans from Stockport are in heaven, they tell me: "We saw him last night...Oh you're in for a treat tonight mate!"

The backslapping continues until about an hour before the great man is due on stage. Then things start to get tense;

"Which songs will HE play?" "What will HE be wearing?"

Yes the devotion stretches this far. And the gig.......well I've seen him 10 times now and this was the best. The songs are taken from the last three albums and, oh, oh, he plays two SMITHS songs!

As the opening bars of 'Paint a Vulgar Picture' ring out grown men are going weak at the knees and when he plays 'Trouble Loves Me' people go wild - understandably.

Long live Moz - long live love!

Richard Felton

MORRISSEY: Disciples flocked to see him.

Photo acknowledgments
Front page photo: © the author. Newspaper cutting courtesy: Ormskirk Advertiser Series. Tattooed girl fan: © Priscilla Grunauer. Tattooed fan Sunderland Empire: © of author. Female fan with placard: © of author. Ring photo: © Dario Rios. Chapter 1: All photos © of author /Ian Latta. Chapter 2: Photo © Cheryl Morris. Chapter 3: Photos © Joy Watson/© of author. Chapter 4: Photo © of author. Chapter 5: Photo © of author. Chapter 6: All photos © Joe Namsinh. Chapter 7: All photos © Jake Atkinson (with the help of Linder Sterling). Chapter 8: All photos © Christine Freeland. Chapter 9: Photo courtesy and © of HMV. Chapter 10: Photo © Johanna Wroe. Chapter 11: All photos © Danny Ibison. Chapter 12: All photos © Mike Coy. Chapter 13: Photo © Jane Rodriguez. Chapter 16: Photo © Martin Bissett. Chapter 18: Photo © Lio Monk. Chapter 19: All photos © Melinda Frank. Chapter 20: Meeting Morrissey photos © David Tseng. Tattoo picture © Melissa Izzo. Chapter 21: All photos © Abrahan Garza, Chapter 22: All photos © Jeff Locher. Chapter 23: Photo © of author. Chapter 24: All photos © Tom Hastings. Chapter 25: Photo © Tom Lennon. Chapter 26: Photo © Iain O'Connor. Chapter 27: All photos © April Richardson. Chapter 28: All photos © Brian Bourguignon. Chapter 29: Photo © David Reyes. Chapter 30: All photos courtesy and © Or Alterman. Chapter 31 © Lake. Back cover photos: left © Jake Atkinson, right © Peter Melis, hug photo © Nicholas Gjoka.

World of Morrissey **99**

3 : Dundee : 1985
2 : Wilmslow : 1985
4 : Altrincham : 1988
5 : Manchester : 1990
7 : Warrington : 1992
9 : London : 1994
10 : Manchester : 1994
11 : Manchester : 1994
12 : Manchester : 1994
14 : Manchester : 1994
15 : Alderley Edge : 1995
16 : Bowdon : 1999
23 : Manchester : 2003
31 : Hale : 2009
18 : Oporto : 1999
30 : Tel Aviv : 2008